IT'S MY CHOICE

JUNIOR BAPTISMAL GUIDE

STEVE CASE

TEACHER'S MANUAL

REVIEW AND HERALD® PUBLISHING ASSOCIATION
HAGERSTOWN, MD 21740

The author assumes full responsibility for the accuracy of all facts
and quotations as cited in this book.

Texts credited to NIV are from the *Holy Bible, New International Version.*
Copyright © 1973, 1978, 1984, International Bible Society. Used by permission
of Zondervan Bible Publishers.

This book was
Edited by Jeannette R. Johnson
Cover designed by Bryan Gray
Typeset: 11/13.5 Helvetica

PRINTED IN U.S.A.

00   5 4 3 2

R&H Cataloging Service
Case, Steve, 1957-
     It's my choice.

     1. Baptism—Handbooks, manuals, etc.   2. SDA—Doctrinal
and controversial works.   3. Baptism—Examinations, questions, etc.
I. Title.

                        265.13

ISBN 0-8280-1094-3

CONTENTS

INTRODUCTION

After more than 15 years of preparing young people for baptism into the Seventh-day Adventist Church, I'm convinced that a pastor's individualized Bible studies hit the mark better than prefab Bible studies. Studies that come straight from the pastor are personal and living rather than automated and sterile, not to mention that most pastors believe their own Bible studies are superior to the prefab versions!

SO WHY PUBLISH ANOTHER SET OF PREFAB BIBLE STUDIES? The driving motivation for creating this particular set of Bible studies grew out of a lack of age-appropriate Bible studies for 10- to 12-year-old young people, the age when most who grow up in the Seventh-day Adventist Church are baptized.

Most adults readily recognize that a child doesn't think in the same way as an adult, but few understand the thinking process and ability of children. As a result, adults write simplified versions of adult Bible studies. The result is something like trying to teach a paraplegic how to drive. Exhorting the person to "try harder" won't speed up or slow down the car. Urging the person to overcompensate in what he/she *can* do, such as gripping the steering wheel more tightly, won't work either. The person needs a specialized vehicle—one with accelerator and brake levers that can be operated by his/her hands.

FIRST THE BLADE . . . These studies are based on the assumption that they are but one piece in the overall religious training of young people. Students who aren't aware of the more common Bible stories may need some basic background prior to beginning these Bible studies. Their ability to find Bible texts is also a helpful prerequisite, since each study has five Bible texts to look up in one's own Bible. Additional material may be supplemented as necessary to round out the student's religious background.

Many children in the church have a rich spiritual background as a result of family training, years of participating in Sabbath school and church, and/or attending a Seventh-day Adventist school. For them, baptism is the next logical step in their spiritual development. "First the stalk, then the head, then the full kernel in the head" (Mark 4:28, NIV).

Spiritual development needs to continue after baptism, too. *A Reason to Believe,* a baptismal preparation guide for teens (edited by Chris Blake [Review and Herald® Pub. Assn., 1993]), is appropriate for the adolescent years, even if a person has already been baptized. If the church doesn't foster continued spiritual development as young people mature, baptizing them at this time is a shortsighted undertaking.

This series of 10 studies explores the 27 fundamental beliefs and 13 baptismal vows of the Seventh-day Adventist Church, and targets the understanding of most 10- to 12-year-olds. As each student continues to mature, additional Bible study should be offered in a search for deeper meanings, based on the learner's receptivity and level of understanding.

SPECIAL TOOLS . . . Each study includes five Bible passages for the student to paraphrase. This can be very difficult. Be patient in assisting the young student in going beyond simply reading the verses to actually understanding their message. The effort spent developing this ability may well be more valuable than anything else learned in the studies and can become a reference source for future use. Be sure to include this activity in each study.

A number of illustrations call for live demonstrations. These are a key part of this curriculum—they give understanding to the students. While this requires advance preparation and sometimes a financial investment on the part of the presenter, it significantly increases the understanding of the student and makes the lesson more memorable. Of course, you may substitute your own activities for the ones suggested in this guide, but do use them! Such demonstrations might not be as necessary for adults, but they are vital for young people.

TEAMING UP WITH OTHERS . . . When a baptismal class consists of students who attend the same church school, the presenter can work in conjunction with the schoolteacher to integrate some of the activities into the school day. For example, one of the baptismal class activities could actually be conducted earlier in the day as a school art project, or a school party can double as an active learning portion of the Bible study.

The home plays a vital role in the spiritual development of young people. Each lesson in the student workbook includes a "family talk back" work sheet, a set of questions intended to assist parents in sharing their personal spiritual journey and faith development. Each can appreciate the steps along the way of others within the family.

We recommend that the final study be conducted in a home setting, even if your students are part of a school baptismal study group. The focus of the final study is the baptismal vows. This rite of passage for 10- to 12-year-olds should be another chapter in their home experience, not separate from it. Others in the family have the opportunity to recognize this rite of passage and renew their own baptismal vows, or look forward to their own baptism in the future.

WHAT ABOUT THE CONTENT? The process of understanding is the unique element in these Bible studies. The theology is traditional Seventh-day Adventism—no new theology and no attempt to ignore certain Adventist teachings, such as the sanctuary.

• Creation (including the Sabbath) is treated as a literal, seven-day event.

- The doctrine of tithe identifies the "storehouse" as the church.
- The Spirit of Prophecy is part of the teaching of spiritual gifts, with added emphasis given to its evidence among God's last-day people.

Because each teacher of the Bible has a unique presentation of biblical truth, each person could probably find some exception to these studies. Should you encounter such an exception, modify the study to fit your armor. Even I adapt these studies for whatever the specific setting might be, and I'm the author! I would expect that others who use this material would use it as a *tool* for Bible study, not as the Bible itself.

It is my prayer that you will use your version of these studies to lead others to Scripture, where they will discover, understand, and accept Jesus, and find life everlasting as a result of that relationship.

HOW TO USE THE

IT'S MY CHOICE STUDENT'S WORKBOOK

It's My Choice Student's Workbook is a companion book to *It's My Choice Teacher's Manual,* a set of 10 age-appropriate Bible studies for 10- to 12-year-old young people. There are three sheets for each of the 10 studies—a Scripture Sheet, a Work Sheet, and a Family Talk Back Sheet. (Samples of each of these workbook sheets for each of the lessons are included in the *It's My Choice Teacher's Manual.*)

SCRIPTURE SHEET. This sheet lists the five texts used in the study. Some people can quickly memorize Scripture. The purpose of this paraphrase sheet is to help the student *understand* each text by putting it into his/her own words. The next step is applying the biblical truth the student is coming to understand. Teachers and parents are encouraged to assist the students in developing this thinking skill by offering a few examples to stimulate the young person's thinking in this direction. Applications should have a primary emphasis on personal application, rather than applying to everyone else!

WORK SHEET. This sheet contains questions and exercises pertinent to the study. The Work Sheet is designed to stimulate thinking and material for group discussion. While this is intended for use in the baptismal class setting, students who are part of a class at church or school will also benefit from discussing these issues at home, perhaps in a family worship setting.

FAMILY TALK BACK SHEET. Seven questions for family discussion offer each person in the family an opportunity to share insights, beliefs, and convictions about each study. This can provide additional development for older children who may have already been baptized as they continue to grow in their faith and understanding. It can be the means of planting seeds for younger children as they look forward to their own baptism. It's a great forum for adults to share their own faith journey with their children, including their present understanding, as well as what they recall from their understanding when they were children.

The Family Talk Back Sheet is for family sharing—not quizzing or grilling of the young baptismal candidate. Utilize these questions as a springboard for additional discussions as family members share with each other elements and issues of their faith journey and experience.

While this is only a tool for families to communicate with each other about spiritual topics, I recommend that each family member put advance thought and preparation into these discussions, rather than "winging it."

SIMPLIFIED BAPTISMAL VOWS. The official baptismal vows of the church have been developed over many years, with special attention given to each word and its usage. However, most children simply cannot understand this precise, technical language. Because I had to paraphrase the baptismal vows for so many baptismal candidates (of a variety of ages) during nearly two decades of pastoral work with young people, I finally wrote out a simplified version. I'd like to give my thanks to numerous pastors who have reviewed these vows and provided valuable input.

Please understand that these have *not* been voted as official baptismal vows, though they were used in *A Reason to Believe,* the youth baptismal preparation guide for teens. The simplified vows are included here because this Bible study material primarily targets the preteen group. To promote understanding and growth, I recommend that students study the official vows side by side with the simplified vows.

May the many 10- to 12-year-old young people who make a commitment for baptism have an understanding of their commitment through the use of these studies. May they continue to grow in their faith during their adolescence and beyond is my prayer.

I Think I'm Ready to Be Baptized . . .

She studies your expression, ready to say "I do" after each vow. But is she *really* ready to be baptized? Or does she simply know the appropriate response and when to say it?

An anxious parent approaches you. "Pastor, will you please visit my son? I think it's time for him to be baptized. Soon he'll enter adolescence, and I'm afraid that if he's not baptized now, perhaps he never will be. Being baptized might be an anchor point for him through the turbulent teen years."

In her third baptismal class, Sandy can't always find the scriptural passages, especially those in the minor prophets or the Epistles. She usually can read the passage without any trouble, but when asked to paraphrase it she draws a blank. However, she says she loves Jesus and wants to be baptized.

Most pastors have experienced these types of situations. And no matter what we decide to do, we're usually left with a twinge of guilt and promise ourselves that we'll handle it better next time. But the next time interrupts us before we've given significant thought to the matter, and the storehouse of pastoral guilt receives another offering. Only a few pastors have the luxury of turning over these predicaments to a youth pastor.

During my internship I had a number of childhood baptismal preparation experiences. I hoped to resolve some of the issues raised during my study at the seminary. During my first quarter I took Salvation, a required six-hour class. This heightened my understanding and appreciation for Jesus and the salvation He offers me; before baptism one should at least understand the basic issue of salvation. (I even entertained the thought that perhaps seminary training should be a prerequisite for baptism.) But could the same level of appreciation and sincerity be present without seminary training? For that matter, is sincerity more important than knowledge? How can one accurately measure sincerity?

WHEN I WAS BAPTIZED . . . My own baptism had an embarrassingly low level of sincerity, primarily because when I was sincere (when my friends were being baptized), I wasn't old enough to be baptized. My parents had determined that I should wait until the age of 12, since that was when Jesus went to the Temple. Even though I attended church each Sabbath, I could *not* enter the temple of the baptismal font with my friends because at the time I was only 11 years old.

My baptism came a year later. A prankster friend had secretly put my name on a baptismal request form and placed it in the offering plate. The pastor followed up on this request with one brief session with me. My parents were active church leaders, and I had been through more than one baptismal class at the Adventist elementary school, so I was considered safe to baptize. For my part, I just wanted to get it over with so I could have some of the "food" during the Communion services that always went way past lunchtime.[1]

On the day of my baptism, the pastor paraded me in front of the congregation as a model of somebody willing to stand alone for Jesus, rather than following the crowd or needing friends to take the plunge with me. I remember thinking how out of touch he was with me, actually proclaiming the very opposite of what was my real situation.

WHAT IS NECESSARY TO BE BAPTIZED? Perhaps in its pristine form, baptism symbolizes a new birth for a believer and is bestowed at the time of the experience it signifies. In this regard, the New Testament story of Philip and the Ethiopian eunuch presents a model emulated in some churches.[2] Saul had three days of blindness and fasting between his Damascus road experience and his baptism.[3]

Today people who meet Christ face-to-face and are converted demonstrate their new birth with baptism.[4] This symbolizes their experience nicely. It's as if they were headed one direction in life, and now they've done an about-face and are going in the opposite direction. Their old selves have died and are buried; they have been resurrected to a new life in Christ.[5]

Christians who join the Adventist Church need not be baptized if their previous denominational affiliation practiced immersion. Though their change in church affiliation is more likely a "new step" in their Christian experience rather than a "new birth" of starting their life with Christ, we apply the same symbol of baptism.

What type of change is necessary for someone who grows up in the community of faith? Having nurtured them in the church, do we really want them to turn around and go the opposite direction?[6] Only 12 percent of our young people can even name a specific moment (a Damascus road experience) in which they made a commitment of their lives to Jesus, while twice that many claim to have maintained a commitment to Jesus from their earliest memory. Three times as many report that their commitment to Jesus developed over a period of time rather than at one specific moment.[7] Yet baptism is the symbol they are to experience to demonstrate that they belong to Christ and His church. At what stage in their development should the symbol be implemented?

Some would emphasize the instruction from the gospel commission that has baptism occurring between "making disciples" and "teaching everything Jesus commanded." While it may be debated whether the elements of Matthew 28:19, 20 are sequential or simultaneous, making disciples is a lengthy process of ups and downs,[8] and one wonders if it is possible even to know everything Jesus commanded[9] or if that would be adequate.[10]

In practice we seem to follow a commonsense approach. A person must be old enough to be accountable and to respond to a general body of information regarding one's acceptance of Jesus as Saviour and Lord, and join the body of Christ known as the Seventh-day Adventist Church.

I THINK . . . Thinking begins before an individual ever considers the philosophical world of Descartes ("I think, therefore I am"). Swiss developmental psychologist Jean Piaget opened new vistas in understanding a person's capacity to think at various stages of his/her cognitive development. While educators receive formal instruction in these matters, pastors rarely are aware of them. But the implications are profound, especially in the arena of baptismal preparation, which, for Adventists, tends to focus on cognition.[11] Piaget identifies four stages of cognitive development.

Stage 1: For the first two years of life an individual's cognition is based on exploration of the world through his or her senses. Discernment comes through placing objects, any objects, into one's mouth, banging things together or on the floor, watching an object being moved about the room and noticing whether the object remains the same or is changed as a result of its change in location. Sitting up, crawling, walking, climbing, and running are also means of discovery. Adults may chuckle to consider this the thinking process of babies and toddlers, but most would agree that it is developmentally appropriate for that age group. We wouldn't seriously consider the stage 1 level of cognitive development adequate for mental assent to baptism unless its purpose was merely to splash and play in the water.

Stage 2: During the next five years (approximately ages 2 to 7) a child's thinking can operate independently from the rest of the body's senses, as was so obvious in the first stage. During this time a child's imagination seems to know no boundaries, as simple objects like a pencil or block of wood can be transformed instantly into a plane, a dog, a banana, and/or a shooting star. This is the age span in which you might purchase a $50 toy and be amazed that the child spends more time playing with the box the toy came in. Chances are, the expensive toy limits the child's creativity, but the simple box requires a vivid imagination to transpose it into whatever the child's thoughts might be.

Not surprisingly, the child's thinking is quite inaccurate. Space relationships aren't fully understood—tall is big, and large is valuable. A child in stage 2 is likely to think a tall, slender glass will hold more water than a short, broad glass, even though their volume might be identical or the volume of the short glass even greater. If asked to choose between a nickel and a dime, the stage 2 child will pick a nickel because it's bigger, assuming therefore that it's more valuable.

Gullibility also characterizes a child in stage 2. Santa Claus is a real person. So is the tooth fairy. Singing animals at pizza parlors or on television are real too.[12] Imaginary playmates and guardian angels are easily understood and entertained. Stage 2 thinkers find the Bible story of Balaam's donkey and the great fish that swallowed Jonah to be completely appropriate ways for God to communicate to selfish, disobedient prophets. Miracles are entirely credible to these minds, in contrast to some "learned adults" who react with skepticism. Daniel and John saw some strange beasts in vision—stage 2 children can *draw* them. Would you like to know what heaven really looks like? A stage 2 child can tell you in detail and with confidence. Certainly no problem is too big for God to handle; just pray about it.

Many Sabbath school teachers in the children's division tap into these creative, imaginative minds and build faith in God as a result. Some parents, especially mothers, almost instinctively seem to know that this wild imagination is appropriate—and temporary. But most would not consider such childlike faith to include adequate mental assent or personal accountability to be baptized.

Stage 3: From approximately the age of 7 until the age of 11 (or even later) a child's cognitive ability centers on what is concrete and tangible. What is real is what

13

is experienced. Flying elephants aren't real; they're just something shown in cartoons or with special effects. Puppets aren't real; they've probably operated them themselves by this time and know that other humans manipulate the form into doing whatever they choose. Santa Claus isn't real; nobody came down their chimney, if they even had one. And they've probably seen four different Santa Clauses at one shopping mall, all at the same time. The tooth fairy isn't real either. It was Mom who tried to sneak a dollar under the pillow in exchange for a dislodged primary tooth.

As relieved as adults might be that the child has become more realistic, the realism comes with a certain loss. If what is real is what is experienced, is God real? Have you seen Him face-to-face? I'm not referring to a homeless person being Jesus to you. The preacher says that Jesus is in heaven interceding on our behalf. If He's in heaven, how can He simultaneously be the homeless person? And if that particular homeless person is Jesus, we're in trouble.

What is heaven like, if it even exists? I want to see photographs, not an artist's rendering. And what good is prayer? I've prayed for a lot of things that I never got. If God's going to pick and choose which prayers He says yes to, why even bother? Besides, I've had some good things happen that I didn't even pray for.

Although some childish perspectives drop away, the stage 3 years are a fertile time for information storage. This is when memorization is quick and trivia sticks. Bible quizzes pitting the boys against the girls make standard Sabbath school fodder. Bible sword drills prepare children to locate scriptural passages quickly—and even read them—but rarely will the child be able to tell you what the passage was about after reading it. What matters is being the first one to find it, not what it says. Come next Sabbath and maybe the boys will finally beat the girls!

Facts are what knowledge is all about. Thinking only in concrete terms makes a stage 3 person unable to reason from principle to application. "Loving God" must be spelled out in concrete terms. The same is true for "loving your neighbor." The Ten Commandments can be appreciated because they are so straightforward, but the Sermon on the Mount, with all the changes and multiple applications, is a bit confusing.

Legalism is natural in this stage of thinking.[13] A stage 3 thinker might sharply denounce you for going 56 miles per hour when the posted speed limit is 55. If aware that the police will write you a ticket for breaking the law, this child would be happy to turn you in. Safety is understood as 55 miles per hour, not as the interaction of the driver(s), the vehicle(s), and the environmental conditions. Good people know their memory verses; bad people don't. And bad people are the ones who don't have special Sabbath clothes (like we have) to wear to church.

In stage 3, symbols cannot be understood. Consider the cross, for example. When you share passionately what the cross means to you, a stage 3 young person is amazed that somebody can get so emotional about two pieces of wood. The Communion service is tasteless wheat crackers with only enough juice for a teasing swallow. And baptism is an embarrassing dunking in which you get your hair all wet, the baptismal robe is certain to float up while you go under, and all the adults smile while you go through this awkward experience.

Stage 3 young people are far too smart to tell you these things. They have memorized acceptable responses to most questions a pastor would pose. They can tell you that the cross is "the manifestation of God's supreme sacrifice, demonstrated through the shed blood of the Lamb as a propitiation for our sins." The Communion service provides "the emblems of Christ's broken body and spilled blood, which enable us to show the Lord's death till He cometh." Baptism is "a symbol of the death, burial, and resurrection of Christ, in which the new believer participates as a testimony of his/her rebirth to newness of life." Many adults, especially pastors, are amazed at the correctness and vocabulary that such young people are able to parrot back. Enamored at hearing their own phraseology, most pastors assume that their teachings have found root in fertile soil.[14]

Stage 3 thinking is the most common stage in which a person is baptized if he or she has grown up in the Adventist Church. These young people are able to master the facts necessary for admission. They aren't able to understand the rich symbolism of the faith, but they're smart and quick enough to know the correct answers to make adults think they do. They don't ask "Why?" all the time. Their most difficult questions have to do with whether or not we will need wings to fly in heaven, and if our pets will be there. Most pastors can soothe such inquirers simply by demonstrating adequate concern and treating these questions with seriousness, which is the spirit in which they are posed.

Stage 4: Stage 4 thinking comes gradually. It may begin as soon as 11 years of age, but for most it happens sometime during the teen years. Physiologically, the left and right half of the brain fuse together. The person is finally able to think about thinking! Logic and abstract thought become possible, and symbols can finally be understood instead of only being memorized.

Because this process occurs gradually, it adds to the upheaval of adolescence.[15] A major factor that makes the junior high years so challenging for many adults to deal with is that while some of their charges are still thinking only in concrete ways, others are eagerly exploring stage 4 thinking with its potential for logic and symbolism. The teacher or youth leader is faced with offering concrete concepts for the stage 3 thinkers, which bores the new stage 4 thinkers, or challenging the new logic of the stage 4 young people and completely losing those still in stage 3.

How can you tell when a person is moving into stage 4 thinking? Probably the most obvious indicator is the onset of questioning. Everything is "Why?"[16] While this can threaten some people, it's simply normal development in a person's thinking. Rather than preventing, ignoring, or disdaining this questioning, it is best to encourage it so that issues can be discussed and developed within the home, church, or school. Suppression will only ensure they are discussed outside of the arena of adult input.[17]

Another indicator that a person has moved into stage 4 thinking is the ability to understand and use puns. While this can be more annoying than persistent questioning, it indicates that a person can think beyond the obvious to new possibilities. Puns are a play on words that can have more than one meaning. Each language has puns, but they generally lose their meaning if they are translated from one language to another. An example in English is "What is gray, about the size of a large dog, howls at the moon at night, and is made of cement?" Most people won't know. They would think of a wolf, but won't mention it because they know that wolves aren't made of cement. Finally, when they give up and are told that it *is* a wolf, they protest, "You said it was made of cement!" The retort? "I just gave that clue to make it hard."

A few people will groan to indicate that they understand this pun. Many won't catch it even after you explain that the pun is a play on the word "hard"—you made it hard (difficult) to guess the object by saying it was made of cement (a hard substance).[18]

The implications for baptismal preparation and one's relationship with God go far beyond telling jokes, however. For the first time young people are finally ready to understand what adults have been telling them for so many years. A conversation with a teen at home on a Sabbath morning might go something like this.

Parent: "Hurry up and get ready for church, or we'll be late!"

Teen: "I'm not going to church today."

Parent: "What do you mean, you're not going to church today?"

Teen: "I just don't know why we go to church on Sabbath anyway."

Parent: "Because God created it on the seventh day, and because we've always observed it in our family. And we're going to observe it again today."

Teen: "But how do we know that people didn't mess up the calendar sometime and we're all doing this on the wrong day anyway?"

Parent: "What are you talking about? Didn't they teach you any better than that at the academy? And what's wrong with your Sabbath school teachers? They're supposed to give you all the answers to these kinds of things. Haven't you been listening when I've taught you all this stuff ever since you were a child?"

To answer the parent's questions, yes, the teen probably has heard all the right answers at home, at church, and at the academy. But the problem was that at the time he or she wasn't capable of understanding. The teen is finally ready to understand what others have been trying to convey for years. These are the teachable moments. Capitalize on them!

We must expect—and anticipate—that sometime during adolescence young people trained in Adventism will need to be "retreaded" with the truths of the faith. They are finally able to think about what they have been taught and possibly even what they've memorized but haven't understood.

To simply baptize a person in stage 3 thinking and then not have time for him or her until he or she becomes a significant adult in the congregation is inviting the adolescent to leave the church. His or her normal development doesn't fit with adult priorities. We liked the parroted answers from stage 3, but are threatened by stage 4 challenges, perhaps because they push us beyond our own thinking as well. If we aren't willing, and even eager, to entertain stage 4 thinking, we shouldn't abuse young people by baptizing them in stage 3 and leaving them to encounter stage 4 and their need for "retreading" with no involvement from us.

I can remember walking alone down the hallway of my academy in the middle of my teen years when an entirely new thought blared into my consciousness—*The Desire of Ages.* Sure, it was a book frequently read and referred to at home. I'd even read it as a requirement for a class. But for the first time I realized why it was called

The Desire of Ages—because it's about Jesus, who is the desire of all ages! That's why it's called *The Desire of Ages!*

While some may laugh at the simplicity of this discovery, it demonstrates the need for the retreading of what is familiar. I was so excited about my epiphany that my mind raced to other titles in the Conflict of the Ages Series. *Patriarchs and Prophets*—I wondered what was in that book. Could it be? It *was!* Can you *believe* it? *Patriarchs and Prophets* is about patriarchs and prophets! If that's true, then *Steps to Christ* must be about . . . *the steps one takes in coming to Christ!*

The only thing more incredible than the simplicity of this discovery was the degree of my excitement about learning these memorized elements and internalizing them. I was finally able to think in new ways, namely, in stage 4 thinking. Now when people shared their passion for "the cross," I could enter into and appreciate their passion because I could finally understand symbols and the richness they provide.

WHEN SHOULD I BE BAPTIZED? In light of cognitive development, an obvious question is Should we postpone commitments such as baptism until there is evidence that stage 4 thinking is at least under way?[19]

The answer is no! First of all, baptism is not just a cognitive experience. It is affective and social in that it involves the person becoming a member of the community of faith. It is also personal. And while it requires total commitment, it is also a beginning of life more than a culmination of it.

Requiring stage 4 thinking for baptism would preclude some from ever being baptized, since some people *never* reach this stage, even in adulthood. How smart (cognitively developed) must you be to give your life and devotion to Jesus?

Since the issue deals primarily with young people who grow up in the Adventist Church, it would be helpful to take an overview of the meaning of baptism, including what it means to those who have been "born Adventist," realizing that only a small percentage (less than 15 percent) will experience a Damascus road conversion experience.

WHAT BAPTISM HAS MEANT . . . Baptism was used as a ceremonial cleansing for proselytes into Judaism. A Gentile could become one of God's people by being baptized. John the Baptist expanded this symbol by introducing a baptism for repentance and for the forgiveness of sins.[20] This included not only Gentiles but also Jews. Evidently, the symbol of baptism can mean more than one thing and can be applied to more than one group of people.

Baptism for the New Testament church following the ascension of Christ, as initiated on the day of Pentecost, was for the forgiveness of sins *and* the reception of the gift of the Holy Spirit.[21]

The Church Fathers added their own twists to the symbol of baptism. Some promoted infant baptism, since a person must be born of water and of the Spirit to enter the kingdom of God.[22] Others took the opposite extreme and suggested that sins couldn't be forgiven after baptism. As a result, some people planned for deathbed baptisms so that there would be no possible way to sin after baptism. They could simply breathe their last and be assured of heaven, since baptism was their final event of life.[23]

Today baptism includes not only the commitment of one's life to Jesus but also membership into the Seventh-day Adventist Church. This usually entails a baptismal preparation class in which the doctrines of the church are presented for cognitive assent.

For young people baptism means different things at different stages of their development. In the sixth grade, a common period for baptism, SDA young people are more likely to think baptism leads to a right relationship with God than to think of baptism as a public statement of faith. By the tenth grade, past the peak years for baptism, the opposite is true: the majority think baptism is a public statement of faith, while a minority think of baptism as leading to a right relationship with Christ.[24]

This shouldn't come as a surprise. For those who grow up in the Adventist Church, baptism has come to be a rite of passage, a type of bar/bas mitzvah. By withholding church membership until this point, regularly attending young people are led to believe that baptism is the doorway through which they become full participants in the life of the church. For this ceremony they are paraded in front of everyone, the congregation affirms their decision by an audible and/or visible vote; the pastor has invested some time with them and now gives them certificates; and congratulations come from people who may have never spoken to them in all their previous years at the church.[25]

I heartily endorse an entire group of friends being baptized together, although at one time I castigated such an action as succumbing to peer pressure. If baptism is not only a symbol of the forgiveness of sins but also a joining to the community of faith, it's better to have established groups of friends joining together, thereby fusing the entire group into the church rather than fragmenting it into members and nonmembers. Baptism is more than a personal decision; it affects a person's relationships and the entire church.

Should a person be baptized before stage 4 thinking begins? It's fine if he/she is, provided he/she is making a commitment of his/her life to Jesus and recognizes that this symbol includes personal and primary responsibility for one's spiritual life. Parents, teachers, and other church people will still influence the new church member, but the primary responsibility will be on the baptized member, who has now chosen what the adults had been choosing for him/her up to that point. Just remember that a "retreading" will be necessary, probably sometime during adolescence.

HOW TO PREPARE STAGE 3 THINKERS . . . The purpose of these baptismal study guides is to present Seventh-day Adventist doctrines at a stage 3 level of thinking. This means the guides must be concrete, rather than symbolic. One study (which includes baptism and the ordinances of the church) focuses solely on symbols. While stage 3 thinkers can't understand this, they can quickly memorize the information. This makes it readily available for future reference.

One of the keys in going beyond memorized, "pat" answers is to have participants paraphrase the correct answers they might easily parrot back to you. That's why each study includes a participant's section for paraphrasing the five key Scripture passages in that study. This can be a challenge for stage 3 thinkers. Resist the temptation just to give them the "right" answers. Lead them to think through what words and phrases mean. It's almost like teaching people to sound out letters as they begin to read words. Be patient. This is a critical process for participants to begin to understand the Bible on a personal level. And in addition to their memorable experiences and newfound ability to understand Scripture for themselves, participants get to keep their written material for future reference.

Each study includes elements especially geared for concrete thinking, identified under the "materials needed" section on the first page of each study. Usually, this requires some advance planning, such as getting props for an illustration instead of just describing it by using words. This can be bothersome, especially for those who have little time to prepare for the studies. However, besides reaching the participant at the appropriate level of thinking, getting the props also communicates that you've taken this study seriously enough to put in the time to prepare.

Hopefully, these study guides will help make baptism truly an appropriate transition of spiritual responsibility as young people continue their development in Christ and in His church. And you have the resources to prepare your stage 3 thinkers for baptism properly.

---

[1] Seventh-day Adventists practice open Communion, meaning that regardless of denominational affiliation (or lack of it), anyone who desires to participate may. In practice, our open Communion is open only to adults. Sometimes an adult will have to take the emblems and give them to a child who desires to participate; otherwise, the deacons might refuse the child's attempt or request to participate. While children are unable to understand the symbolism of the Communion service, as is explained later in this article, they do understand being included or excluded from church activities, as well as rites of passage.

[2] See Acts 8:35-38. Consider the practice of most Baptist churches.

[3] See Acts 9:4-6, 9, 17, 18. Ananias was sent by God to restore Saul's sight and to pronounce the infilling of the Holy Spirit. Saul's new birth was not in the matter of becoming religious (see Acts 22:3-5), but in accepting Jesus as the Messiah, the Son of God (see Acts 9:20-22).

[4] See John 3:3-7 and Acts 2:37-39.

[5] See Romans 5:3, 4; 2 Corinthians 5:17.

[6] See Horace Bushnell's *Christian Nurture,* first published in 1861 by Charles Scribner, now available from Baker Book House. Perhaps the most used quotation is "The child is to grow up a Christian, and never know himself as being otherwise" (p. 10).

[7] Based on unpublished data from Valuegenesis regarding the time of one's commitment to Jesus.

[8] For example, see Matthew 4:18-20; 8:23-26; 10:1; 16:15-19; 23; 26:21, 22, 35, 56, 74.

[9] See John 21:25.

[10] See John 16:12, 13.

[11] For more regarding Piaget's theory of cognitive development, see "J. Piaget's Theory," in P. H. Mussen, ed., *Carmichael's Manual of Child Psychology,* 3rd ed. (New York: John Wiley and Sons, 1970), vol. 1; George and Meriem Fair Kaluger, *Human Development: The Span of Life,* 3rd ed. (St. Louis: Times Mirror/Mosby, 1984); Robert E. Clark, Joanne Brubaker, and Roy B. Zuck, *Childhood Education in the Church,* (Chicago: Moody Press, 1986).

[12] Some well-meaning but hypersensitive adults equate a child's imagination with only evil. Because of this, they attempt to shield their children from unrealistic elements such as talking animals, flying elephants, and even puppets. What they don't realize is that children will naturally think in such unrealistic ways even though they are shielded, and they will grow out of this at the next stage of thinking even if they continue to be exposed to the unrealistic world of the imagination.

[13] Because stage 3 thinking is not limited to ages 7 to 11, this may be part of the explanation for legalism in the church. Adults are quite capable of thinking in stage 3 terms, resulting in a crippling legalism that can affect many. Don't assume that once a person reaches the age of 11 that legalism will pass. Although it would be nice, there are too many adults fixated in this stage to believe that. The ages

of 7 to 11 are suggestive only of what is normal development. Some older people are simply "retarded" in their thinking; their development has ceased.

[14] To discover if your youngster really understands what he/she is parroting back, try having him/her paraphrase his/her articulate phrase and see if he/she can come up with something more original than a tried-and-true cliché. Of course, this should be done in a nonthreatening way.

[15] While puberty is a major transitional phenomenon that usually marks the onset of adolescence, stage 4 thinking certainly exacerbates the upheaval. Stage 4 thinking makes possible the "imaginary audience" in which the person is able to think of the possibility that other people are thinking about him/her. In fact, there is probably an entire (imaginary) audience looking at me right now! How embarrassing!

[16] Small children also ask why, but do so at a very elementary level or simply to get your attention. They may ask why during the middle of your response, just to be sure you will continue to focus on them. When adolescents ask why, it is either to challenge your authority or because they want a deeper response than has been satisfactory before. They have put away childish things and are preparing to enter adulthood. They want to be equipped with the best answers possible. They already know what their parents think on most issues. They're experimenting with other adults before they internalize what their personal values and beliefs will be.

[17] See Roger Dudley, *Passing On the Torch* (Hagerstown, Md.: Review and Herald® Pub. Assn., 1986).

[18] While people are more apt to groan at a pun than laugh at it, those who groan the most are the ones who will use it on others. Don't be surprised if some stage 3 thinkers know the answers to puns. That doesn't mean they understand them. They may be demonstrating their tremendous ability to memorize trivia, and they like the attention they get from telling the joke/pun. To determine if such wise guys really are in stage 4 thinking, see if they can make up puns on their own rather than only repeating ones they've heard before.

[19] Ronald Goldman rocked the religious education community in the 1960s with *Religious Thinking From Childhood to Adolescence* (Routledge and Kegan Paul, 1964) and *Readiness for Religion* (Routledge and Kegan Paul, 1965). Goldman argued that because so much religious instruction is given before a person is capable of understanding it, when the age of understanding comes there is an accompanying rejection of religion because of inoculation from overexposure when a person wasn't ready for adult perspectives. For a response to Goldman, see Iris V. Cully, *Christian Child Development* (Harper and Row, 1979), pp. 143-156; Lawrence O. Richards, *A Theology of Children's Ministry* (Zondervan, 1983), pp. 55-70, 109-129; and Lawrence O. Richards, *The Word Parents' Handbook* (Word, 1983).

[20] See Luke 3:2, 3; Mark 1:4, 5.

[21] See Acts 2:37-39; 19:1-7.

[22] John 3:5. See also George Buttrick, ed., *The Interpreter's Dictionary of the Bible,* vol. 1, p. 352.

[23] See *The Shepherd of Hermas,* as presented in Patrick J. Hamell, *Handbook of Patrology,* pp. 32-34. In an attempt to impose the seriousness of holding to one's commitment to Jesus in light of the imminent persecution and ensuing return of Christ, believers were allowed up to one sin to be forgiven after baptism. Once that outlook is taken, it's not long before baptism is the seal of sinlessness.

[24] Personal communication from Jerome Thayer, Andrews University director of the Seventh-day Adventist religion achievement test program. This test is a measure of the cognitive achievement of young people attending Adventist schools. Actual numbers for grade 6 were:

"In the plan of salvation, baptism is a public statment of faith"—33 percent.

"In the plan of salvation, baptism leads to a right relationship with Christ"—45 percent.

The actual numbers for grade 10 were:

"In the plan of salvation, baptism is a public statment of faith"—64 percent (with the number being lower if the student had fewer years in Seventh-day Adventist schools or if the parents weren't Seventh-day Adventists).

"In the plan of salvation, baptism leads to a right relationship with Christ"—26 percent (with the number being higher if the student had fewer years in Seventh-day Adventist schools or if the parents weren't Seventh-day Adventists).

[25] For many, participation in the Communion service now also becomes possible. But most will find the rite of passage to be somewhat hollow or short-lived when they discover that ownership of the church really is in the hands of the adults. The pastor is not able to continue the focused attention that was necessary for baptismal preparation. For the young people to really be accepted in most churches on a regular basis, they must act like adults rather than as young people. A few will foreclose their identity development to receive such acceptance. Most won't.

A Summary of Piaget's Stages of Cognitive Development

Swiss developmental psychologist Jean Piaget demonstrated that people's thinking (cognition) develops through four stages. This process has implications for what and how we instruct people about God. In brief, Piaget pointed out the following:

STAGE 1 (from birth to 2 years of age).
The senses are the avenue for discovery and understanding.
Objects are handled, observed, listened to, smelled, and tasted.
The mind is able to comprehend that objects maintain their substance even when they are moved to a different location (object permanence).
Most cradle roll division leaders are aware of stage 1 comprehension and provide a variety of objects for the babies and toddlers to feel, see, listen to, smell, and even taste.

STAGE 2 (from approximately 2 to 7 years of age).
The imagination comes alive with fantasy as children think in wildly creative and unrealistic ways.
They are apt to believe almost anything an authority figure tells them. Stories of miracles, heaven, the power of prayer, and divine interventions are very credible to them.

STAGE 3 (from approximately 7 to 11 years of age or older).
Thinking is based on what is concrete. What is real is what is experienced. Memorization is sharp and quick. Symbols cannot yet be understood, although they can be memorized.

STAGE 4 (no sooner than 11 years of age, although it may occur sometime during adolescence).
Logic and abstract thought become possible, characterized by frequently asking "Why?"
Symbols can now be understood.
There is a need for "retreading" what has been memorized previously as the internalization of values and beliefs begins.

Baptismal Bible Study Guide Outline 1

SALVATION AND THE GREAT CONTROVERSY

Introduction: There's a war going on!

I. The beginning of the Bible tells us about it (Genesis 3:15).
    A. Paraphrase of Genesis 3:15.
    B. "Enmity" is showing hatred between two groups.
    C. Between God and Satan.
    D. Affects us today because of the Garden of Eden.

II. All of us have been on Satan's side of the war (Romans 3:23).
    A. Romans 3:23: "All."
    B. Paraphrase of Romans 3:23.

III. The story continues (Romans 6:23).
    A. Romans 6:23: Wages for what you earn.
    B. Romans 6:23: Gift is what someone gives you.
    C. Paraphrase of Romans 6:23.
    D. Activity: Tug-of-war.

IV. Because of Jesus we can now choose our side of the war (1 Kings 18:21, 39).
    A. 1 Kings 18:21, 39 (or Joshua 24:15).
    B. Activity: Computers are to be programmed; no choice.
    C. Paraphrase of 1 Kings 18:21, 39.

V. Assurance of whose side you're on (1 John 5:11-13).
    A. 1 John 5:11-13: A matter of math (you + Jesus = life).
    B. Activity: Token for goods/reward.
    C. Paraphrase of 1 John 5:11-13.

VI. Conclusion: Whose side do you choose to be on?
    A. Mark work sheet.
    B. Sing, "Whose Side Are You Leaning On?"

Baptismal Bible Study Guide 1

SALVATION AND THE GREAT CONTROVERSY

SCRIPTURE TEXTS:
1. Genesis 3:15: There's a war going on!
2. Romans 3:23: All of us have been on Satan's side.
3. Romans 6:23: We earn death; God gives life.
4. 1 Kings 18:21, 39 (Joshua 24:15; Ephesians 6:10-12): We choose whose side we're on.
5. 1 John 5:11-13: You can be sure of your eternal life.

DECISION TIME:
Whose side do you choose to be on in the great controversy?
Seal the decision by singing "Whose Side Are You Leaning On?"

MAKE IT CONCRETE (stage 3 appropriate):
Tug-of-war against a truck with a winch (or a large tree).
Computer with program (can't choose for itself).
Token or certificate for arcade, bus, or food item.

MATERIALS NEEDED:
Basic study tools for each student—Bible, workbook Scripture Sheet 1, workbook Work Sheet 1, pen or pencil.
1 large rope for tug-of-war for the entire group.
Access to truck with a winch or a large tree or other sturdy, stationary object.
A computer with software.
A token or certificate for a local arcade, bus, or food item.

INTRODUCTION:
I have something I'd like to give to each of you. But before I do, you need to be aware of something: there's a war going on! This is more than simply two teams competing in a sporting contest or a longtime rivalry. It's bigger than even World War I or World War II.

I. GENESIS 3:15: THERE'S A WAR GOING ON!
We can read about it in the very first book of the Bible.
(Look up Genesis 3:15 and have one of the students read it. Have another student paraphrase it. Each student can write a paraphrase of it on Scripture Sheet 1.)

Enmity. The King James Version of the Bible (and several other versions) says there is enmity between two people—the serpent, Satan, and the woman, Eve. "Enmity" is our new word for today. Can anyone give me a definition for the word "enmity"?

(Field several definitions, if the students have them.)

According to the dictionary, enmity is "a feeling or demonstration of hatred between two people or groups of people."

(Have students write the definition on their Work Sheet 1, question 1, as you write it on the board.)

That's pretty strong stuff! Did you notice who the two people or groups of people are?

(Field observations, if there are any.)

Verse 15 of Genesis 3 says there will be enmity between "you" and "the woman." The "you" refers to the serpent/Satan, as explained in Genesis 3:14 and Revelation 12:9. In Genesis 3:13 "the woman" refers to Eve. The rest of our verse points out that the enmity will not only be between you and the woman, but between your offspring, or seed, and her offspring, or seed. In other words, the battle continues between the followers of Satan and those who follow Eve and her offspring, who crushes Satan's head. Do you know who deals the deathblow to Satan?

(Field answers from the participants.)

That's right. Jesus dealt Satan the deathblow when He died for us on the cross. Because of that, we can be followers of Jesus instead of naturally and selfishly following Satan.

I find it amazing and encouraging that Eve, the one who first gave in to Satan, is the person God identifies as being the example of God's followers who are against Satan. Plus, the Son of God chose to be born through the family line of Eve, the one who really messed up. It's pretty incredible that God forgives us for such big mistakes and restores us to places of honor we certainly don't deserve. But before we're part of Eve's side against the followers of Satan we must recognize that we've been on Satan's side.

II. ROMANS 3:23: ALL OF US HAVE BEEN ON SATAN'S SIDE.

Let's look at Romans 3:23. It's a familiar text that some of you probably have memorized.

(Have a student read it aloud.)

How many have sinned?

(Allow students to respond and circle the correct answer to question 2 on their Work Sheet 1.)

That's pretty serious! Each of us has been on Satan's side. We've been against God. That means we're really a bunch of losers, because according to the book of Revelation, when it's all over, Jesus and His followers are the winners, while Satan and his followers are the losers.

(Have students write the paraphrase on their Scripture Sheet 1, then have some share their paraphrases of the verse.)

Some people figure that when they face God on the judgment day they'll simply stack up their accumulated list of good deeds and compare it with their accumulated list of bad deeds. As long as the good deeds list is longer, they figure they will get to go to heaven. Their statements sound something like this: "I do more good things than bad things" or "I'm not all that bad." But according to the verse we just read, it's not a matter of balancing good against bad. The payment for sin is death. If you think you're not guilty, you're blind, as we see in our next text, Romans 6:23!

III. ROMANS 6:23: WE EARN DEATH; GOD GIVES LIFE.

The same book of the Bible, Romans, tells us more about this situation. Turn to Romans 6:23, and let's compare the first half of the verse with the second half of the verse.

(Have a student read the first half of the verse aloud.)

Wages are what you get for the work you do; it's what you've earned, what you deserve, what is rightfully yours. What are our wages for sinning?

(Have students respond.)

This certainly isn't good news for us, even though it's what we deserve.

(Have a student read the second half of Romans 6:23 aloud.)

A gift is what somebody gives you because he/she wants to, not because you deserve it. If you deserve it, it's not a gift—it's your wages. What is the gift God offers us?

(Have students respond.)

Eternal life through Jesus. I prefer the gift more than the wages I deserve. How about you?

(Have students respond, giving reasons that they prefer eternal life to the wages of sin. Then have them write their paraphrase on their Scripture Sheet 1, followed by some of them sharing their paraphrases of the verse. Have them write their answer to question 3 on their Work Sheet 1.)

I'd like for you to join me outside as we try out these two sides that are battling it out.

(If there's enough time, the first tug-of-war can be between the students, evenly divided into two groups. One group can be "Satan's followers," and the other group can be "Eve and Jesus' followers.")

Remember, I pointed out that this war, this enmity, is bigger than just people fighting against each other. Supernatural forces are involved too. We'll have this winch on this truck stand for Jesus. Since all of us were born naturally as sinners, we were naturally on Satan's selfish side. So we'll try the tug-of-war against the winch.

(Have all the students join in a tug-of-war against the winch. After they are unable to move the truck, remind them that Jesus is more than simply strong and stable—He's also active and moving. Start up the winch and encourage the students to continue to tug against it even though they don't have a chance. Most will give up because they recognize they have no chance.)

This is what's happening in the real war too. Except we read about one other element—Jesus offers us the gift of being on His side so we can receive eternal life instead of the death we deserve for being on Satan's side. Would any of you like to be on Jesus' side and pull *with* the truck and winch instead of *against* it?

(Let those who would like to be on Jesus' side join for one final pull. If nobody

chooses to pull against Jesus, tie that end of the rope to something so large or strong that the group may need the assistance of the winch to pull it. Have them try to pull against Satan's team by themselves, and then turn on the winch to assist them.)

IV. 1 KINGS 18:21, 39: WE CHOOSE WHOSE SIDE WE'LL BE ON.

Because of what Jesus has already done for us, the only thing that remains is for us to choose to be on His side instead of on Satan's side. This choice has been offered to people repeatedly throughout the history of this earth, and it's offered to you too.

Let's turn to 1 Kings 18:21, 39 *(or you may prefer Joshua 24:15)* to see one example of how this choice has been presented in the past.

(Have one of the students read the text aloud.)

The choice is yours.

We live in the computer age. Computers are able to do incredible things at an extremely fast rate of speed, much faster than humans can. But computers can do only what they're programmed to do.

(Demonstrate or have some of the students demonstrate their power to make computers their servants.)

Computers aren't given the power of choice as to whether or not they want to follow you. If God had wanted to, He could have made us like computers. Instead, He gave us the rewarding—and dangerous—power of choice.

Those who follow God do so because they choose to. Others might have chosen for you to follow God, but you're realizing that you're getting old enough to make a choice yourself. Whose side do you choose—Satan's selfish side, where we all were born, *or* Jesus' side of eternal life? There is no middle ground. The choice of whose side you'll be on is up to you!

(Have students write a paraphrase on their Scripture Sheet 1, then have some of them share their paraphrases of the verse.)

V. 1 JOHN 5:11-13: YOU CAN BE SURE OF YOUR ETERNAL LIFE.

When you choose to be on Jesus' side in the great war, how can you be sure that you really have eternal life? Even when you choose to be on His side, there are times when you're likely to wonder. I have those questions once in a while. When I do, here's the text I turn to: 1 John 5:11-13.

(Have one of the students read verses 11 and 12 aloud.)

It's a matter of basic math. If you have Jesus (the Son), you have life.

(Write on the board: you + Jesus = eternal life.)

If you don't have Jesus (the Son), you don't have life.

(Write on the board: you – Jesus = no life.)

If you have any question or doubt about whether or not you have eternal life, simply pray, "Jesus, I want You in my life." You now have the Son; you now have eternal life.

I told you at the beginning of our Bible study that I had something for you. I do.

(Hand each student a token to a local arcade or for an item of food or a local bus/subway ride.)

26

Just as God offers you eternal life (salvation) because of Jesus' gift of dying on the cross for you, I'm giving you this token as a gift. Although it's not nearly as valuable as eternal life, it is valuable. But it's really worth something only if you take it and use it.

Did you know that some people won't even accept the free gift God offers them? Others will take the gift but won't ever go to the arcade (bus/subway) and use it.

(An ideal follow-up is to take the group to the arcade, especially if adult supervision is required for entrance. The same concept can be implemented with food or drink tokens or certificates and a trip to the business that honors the certificates.)

Some think God's offer is too good to be true. I think that's why John wrote verse 13.

(Have one of the students read verse 13 aloud.)

This was written to those who believe in Jesus so they can know that they have eternal life.

(Have students write a paraphrase on their Scripture Sheet 1, then have some share their paraphrases of the verse.)

CONCLUSION:

So whose side do you choose to be on? The battle continues. You can't be neutral. Will you be on Satan's selfish side and end up losing, or will you choose to be on Jesus' side and receive the gift of eternal life? Mark which side you choose to be on at the bottom of your Work Sheet 1.

(Give the students time to mark their choice.)

Welcome to the battle! There's enmity. You have the choice of which side you will be on. Will those who chose to be on God's side join me in singing "Whose Side Are You Leaning On?"

(Sing the song to close the Bible study.)

SCRIPTURE SHEET 1
Salvation and the Great Controversy

1. Genesis 3:15:

What it means: _____

_____

2. Romans 3:23:

What it means: _____

_____

3. Romans 6:23:

What it means: _____

_____

4. 1 Kings 18:21, 39:

What it means: _____

_____

5. 1 John 5:11-13:

What it means: _____

_____

WORK SHEET 1
Salvation and the Great Controversy

1. What does "enmity" mean?

_____

_____

_____

2. How many people have sinned? (Circle the correct answer.)
   a. Nobody.
   b. Everybody.
   c. About half of the people.
   d. Everybody except me.

3. How does a person get eternal life?

_____

_____

_____

4. Whose side are you on?

   ○ God's side   ○ Satan's side

FAMILY TALK BACK SHEET 1
Salvation and the Great Controversy

1. Have each person identify some place he or she has seen "enmity" (hatred or the war between good and evil, Christ and Satan).

2. Share an example of something you have done when you were on Satan's side (selfishness).

3. Do you do more good things than bad things? Explain.

4. Specifically, how does a person change from Satan's side to God's side?

5. What are examples of "wages" you've earned? What are examples of gifts you've received?

6. After a person joins God's side, does he or she ever do things that make it seem as though he or she is still on Satan's side? Explain.

7. Whose side are you on—Christ's or Satan's? How do you know?

Baptismal Bible Study Guide Outline 2

THE SECOND COMING OF JESUS

Introduction: When you've planned the party, you want to be there!

I. Jesus promised to return (John 14:1-3).
   A. Paraphrase of John 14:1-3.
   B. What will heaven be like?
   C. Art project of what heaven will be like (supply materials).
   D. The best part of heaven is to be with Jesus.

II. How Jesus will come (1 Thessalonians 4:16-18).
   A. He will come with a trumpet blast to get everyone's attention.
   B. Read and paraphrase 1 Thessalonians 4:16-18.
   C. Nobody will miss this event.
   D. Will you be glad or sad when Jesus returns?
   E. Fill in Work Sheet.

III. Events of the millennium (Revelation 20:1-10).
   A. *Millennium* means 1,000 years.
   B. Events that happen during the millennium.
   C. All our questions will be answered.
   D. "For ever and ever."
   E. God dwells with us in the New Jerusalem.

IV. Urgency to spread the gospel (Matthew 24:14).
   A. *Adventists* are people who look forward to the second advent of Jesus.
   B. Read and paraphrase Matthew 24:14.

V. Gospel commission (Matthew 28:19, 20).
   A. All of God's followers get to spread the good news.
   B. Whom would you like to invite to the biggest party in the world?

VI. Conclusion: Make an invitation list for the return of Jesus.

Baptismal Bible Study Guide 2

THE SECOND COMING OF JESUS

SCRIPTURE TEXTS:

1. John 14:1-3: Jesus has given His promise that He will come back to earth for us.
2. 1 Thessalonians 4:16-18: When Jesus comes, everyone will know about it!
3. Revelation 20:1-10: What happens after Jesus returns? Do we just go off to heaven forever?
4. Matthew 24:14: Everybody needs to find out about these things.
5. Matthew 28:19, 20: Jesus asked His followers to take this good news to the whole world—and He'll be with us the whole time!

DECISION TIME:

Do you believe that Jesus will keep His promise to return for us?
List those persons you will invite to be ready for the return of Jesus.

MAKE IT CONCRETE (stage 3 appropriate):

Have a party just before the Bible study.
Create an artist's rendering of a heavenly mansion.
Arrange for someone to give a trumpet blast that can be heard by all the students.
Make a party invitation list of people to invite to be ready for the return of Jesus.

MATERIALS NEEDED:

Basic study tools for each student—Bible, workbook Scripture Sheet 2, workbook Work Sheet 2, pen or pencil.
Party supplies.
Art and craft materials for making a picture of one's heavenly mansion.
Trumpet and trumpet player.
Party invitation list for each student.

INTRODUCTION:

(If possible, conduct the Bible study following a party for all the students. Include party food, games, and prizes. Be sure everyone receives invitations before the party.)
Planning a party takes energy, time, and money to make it happen. Besides sending out invitations, you need to get the food together, plan the games, get prizes and decorations, and get the party place all set up.
After you've done everything it takes to make a party happen, do you think you'd go to the party, or would you just skip it?
(Field responses from students.)
I know that *I* surely wouldn't miss the party! When it means so much to me that

I've planned it and paid for it, you can be sure that I'd be there too.

Do you think that Jesus would miss the biggest party in the world—the one that He put His energy into, the one He has been planning for thousands of years? Do you think He would miss the party that He paid for by dying for us? Of course not! He can hardly wait to celebrate with us!

I. JOHN 14:1-3: JESUS HAS GIVEN HIS PROMISE THAT HE WILL COME BACK TO EARTH FOR US.

(Look up John 14:1-3 and have one of the students read it. Have another student paraphrase it. Each student can write a paraphrase of it on Scripture Sheet 2.)

Do you believe that Jesus came to earth and died for you? Of course, nobody would consider that to be very much fun. But Jesus did it because He loves us so much that He didn't want us to be cut off from Him forever. He came to earth and died for us so that we could eventually go to heaven with Him.

If Jesus went through all of that horrible stuff (being rejected, persecuted, and hung on a cross), don't you think He will come back for the fun part—the celebration in which we get to go to heaven with Him? Not only does that make sense, but He has even given His promise that He will come back for us. That's what we read in John 14:1-3. There's no need for us to get discouraged because we can't see Jesus at this very moment. Because we believe in God, we're looking forward to the return of Jesus.

And there's plenty of room for us in heaven. In fact, according to what we read, Jesus is preparing a place especially for us. Have you ever wondered what that place will be like? Let's use our imaginations a little bit. You know that Jesus knows you so well that He will make a perfect place for you. But what do you think it will look like? Will it be in the city or in the country? In the mountains or by an ocean or lake? What size will it be? What color will it be? Will it be more than one story tall?

Let's take some time right now to create a picture of the type of place we'd like Jesus to prepare for us. I've brought some supplies, and you might already have some things you want to include. Let's get started!

(If this Bible study is being done in a school setting, this could be an art activity that the teacher includes as part of the curriculum. Have a variety of art and craft supplies, such as glue, glitter, Popsicle sticks, feathers, jelly beans, felt material, and even crayons, markers, and paints. Allow as much as 15 minutes for this activity. Move among the students, asking questions about their creations. When the time is up and the supplies have been put away, continue the Bible study with the following segue.)

Of course, our artwork is just an idea of what Jesus is preparing for us. He's a better artist than we are, and He's making sure the place being made for us is ideal. I can hardly wait to see it! How about you?

But there's something even better than our own mansion. The very last part of our text mentioned it: Jesus' desire to be with us. The Bible says that Jesus will come back and take us to heaven so we can be with Him. Just think of it—we've heard about Jesus all of our lives, and now we'll be able to see Him, just like we can see each other right now.

Have you ever wanted to ask Jesus a question and have Him give you an answer right away? You'll be able to do that too. I wonder what it will be like to play tag with Jesus. Do you think He has any incredible computer games? What sports will He want to play? What jokes will He tell? What new places will He show us? What kind of roller coaster do you think He would make? What stories will He tell us? This is going to be great! Do you agree?

II. 1 THESSALONIANS 4:16-18: WHEN JESUS COMES, EVERYONE WILL KNOW ABOUT IT.

(Begin with a loud trumpet blast that will get everyone's attention, such as the lead up to a group shout of "Charge!" So there is a greater element of surprise, it may be best to have someone besides the Bible study leader play the trumpet.)

Did anybody miss that? Perhaps if you were deaf you would have. Maybe you're feeling deaf now! And that's just a human playing a human-made trumpet. Imagine what it will be like when we hear God's trumpet when Jesus returns! Let's read about it in 1 Thessalonians 4:16-18.

(Have a student read the passage and then have several students offer their paraphrase of the passage. Have each student write a personal paraphrase of these verses on Scripture Sheet 2.)

Nobody on earth will miss the return of Jesus. In fact, God's people who have died (the "dead in Christ") will hear what's going on too. They will be resurrected when they hear the shout, the voice of the archangel, and the trumpet of God. There's no secret here! Some might be surprised that Jesus really does exist and that He was true to His promise, but it's not the type of thing that will happen one day and you hear about it in the news the next day. No, it will be impossible to miss this piece of news if you're anywhere on the earth at that time.

(Note also Revelation 1:7—"Every eye will see him"; and Luke 17:24—"The Son of Man . . . will be like the lightning which flashes and lights up the sky.")

Everyone will see it. The only question will be Are you glad or sad that Jesus has returned? For those who have been looking forward to seeing Jesus, this will probably be the happiest day of their lives. For those who are against Jesus, this will be just about the worst day of their lives. The trumpet will sound. By choosing to be on God's side now, that day will be a great one for us! No wonder 1 Thessalonians 4:16-18 ends with the message "Comfort one another with these words."

Let's take a look at our Work Sheet for this lesson. The first question is "What events will happen when Jesus comes the second time?" What are some of the things we've discovered and discussed so far?

(Field responses from students. If they have difficulty coming up with anything, refer back to 1 Thessalonians 4:16-18.)

That's right. When Jesus returns the second time (the first time Jesus came to earth was as a baby about 2,000 years ago; He died for our sins so we can go with Him to heaven when He returns to earth the second time), we can expect the following things to happen:

1. The dead followers of Jesus will be resurrected.

2. Those who aren't followers of Jesus will be killed by the brightness of His coming (2 Thessalonians 1:8-10; 2:8).

3. All of God's people will be taken to heaven.

III. REVELATION 20:1-10: WHAT HAPPENS AFTER THE RETURN OF JESUS? DO WE JUST GO OFF TO HEAVEN FOREVER?

Does anyone know what the word "millennium" means?

(Field responses from students.)

It's a Latin word that means 1,000 years. One chapter in the Bible, almost at the very end, focuses especially on the millennium—the 1,000 years following the second coming of Jesus. Let's turn to Revelation 20 and discover a few of the things that will happen during the millennium and at the end of the millennium. We'll write these things on our Work Sheet for this lesson.

Let's begin with verses 1 through 6 as we answer the question "What events will happen during the millennium?"

(Have students read one verse at a time and offer an explanation. Since the passage uses a lot of symbolic language, this can be challenging for a literal understanding of the key, the bottomless pit/abyss, chain, beast, image, mark, etc. As the group reads through these six verses, keep the focus on the four items that occur during the millennium; otherwise, you'll begin a verse-by-verse paraphrase of the entire book of Revelation—a worthwhile series, but for another time!)

1. Satan is bound to earth (verses 1 and 2).

2. Satan can no longer deceive people—he deserves a vacation (verse 3)!

3. God's people in heaven get to judge whether or not God has been fair and done right (verse 4; see also 1 Corinthians 6:2, 3).

4. Reign with Christ (verse 6).

(Have students write the events on their Work Sheet after question 2.)

Just think, when the millennium is over, all your questions about who's in heaven and who isn't will be answered to your satisfaction! Lots of things we don't have a clue about now will become obvious as we get a complete picture of things.

Sometimes we're tempted to think that people who do good things get to go to heaven and those who do bad things won't be there. Remember our last study? We looked at Romans 6:23 and noticed that each of us deserves to die as the wages for our sins—it's what we've earned. None of us deserves to be in heaven. The only people who will be there will be those who have accepted the gift of eternal life.

Looking back at Revelation 20, let's read verses 7 through 10 to find out what happens at the end of the millennium.

(Have students read these passages, discuss them as a group, and begin to write the events on their Work Sheet after question 3.)

1. Resurrection of those who didn't follow Jesus (verse 5).

2. Satan released to deceive these people again (verse 7).

3. Satan and his followers try to destroy God and His people (verse 9).

4. Fire destroys Satan and his followers (verses 9, 10).

"For ever and ever" at first sounds like eternity. From God's perspective, for ever and ever *is* eternity. But for us, for ever and ever can be for our whole life (which might be 70 or 80 years). And some of us might live only until we're 15 or 20 years old. Our for ever and ever certainly wouldn't be very much like eternity. But whether we live for 15 years or for 80 years, our choice to follow Jesus can indeed last for eternity. Those who choose Jesus will be alive with Him for eternity. Those who choose not to be with Jesus will be dead for eternity.

It sounds terrible, but if those who reject God burn in the fires of hell for eternity, they have eternal life. It would be a horrible eternal life to keep burning for millions and zillions of years, but if they were still alive, they would have eternal life. Obviously, the meaning of for ever and ever for the destruction of those who haven't accepted eternal life is that they will be destroyed for ever and ever—the fact of their destruction will be for eternity, and that includes Satan, too!

But let's not end the study of the millennium on a negative note. Notice the first few verses of Revelation 21 (verses 1-4).

(Have a student read these verses. Let individuals comment about which part of the description of the New Jerusalem especially appeals to them.)

So we have one more line to fill in regarding what happens after the millennium:

5. The New Jerusalem comes to earth, where God dwells with us.

IV. MATTHEW 24:14: EVERYBODY NEEDS TO FIND OUT ABOUT THESE THINGS.

A number of times people have made predictions about exactly when Jesus will return to earth. In fact, just before the Seventh-day Adventist Church got started, there was a tremendous interest in setting the specific date of October 22, 1844, as the date Jesus would return to earth. It's pretty obvious now that He didn't come back at that time. But those who are eager for Jesus to return live their lives as though He could come back anytime, because they are always ready to see Him face-to-face. Because they are so eager for the second advent—the coming of Jesus—they are sometimes referred to as "Adventists."

Are you an Adventist? Are you looking forward to the second advent of Jesus? If you're eager for this grand event to take place, spread the word! In fact, the Bible tells us to share this news with others. Let's read about it in Matthew 24:14.

(Have one student read the text and allow everyone to discuss it before writing their own paraphrase on Scripture Sheet 2.)

The good news is that because of the gift of Jesus we can be on God's side in the great war between Christ and Satan (see lesson 1), and receive the gift of eternal life. When Jesus returns to earth the second time, everyone will know about it. That will be good news for those who have accepted God's gift, but bad news for those who haven't. And just think, we get to spread the good news so others can accept the gift of God too!

V. MATTHEW 28:19, 20: JESUS INSTRUCTED HIS FOLLOWERS TO TAKE THIS GOOD NEWS TO THE WHOLE WORLD, AND HE WILL BE WITH US THE WHOLE TIME!

Some people have the idea that the only people who can tell others the good news about Jesus and His return are the preachers/ministers. Nothing could be further from the truth! All of God's followers can tell others the good news. Don't believe this just because I say it—let's read it in Matthew 28:19, 20. Some people have called this passage the gospel commission, because all of Christ's followers are commissioned, or called, to share this gospel/good news.

(Have one student read this passage aloud while the rest follow along. Discuss what it means and have each student write a paraphrase on Scripture Sheet 2.)

The return of Jesus will be the biggest party in the whole world. He has been planning it for thousands of years. You've been invited, and you also have the opportunity of inviting others! I have a blank invitation list for each of you. You can write the names of the people you'd like to invite to the big party—the return of Jesus.

(Hand a blank list to each student.)

CONCLUSION:

Put your name at the top of the list—you're invited to the party! Do you believe that Jesus will keep His promise to return?

Add at least four more names to your list. These are people you want to receive an invitation to be at the party too. They might be your relatives (parent, sibling, grandparent, etc.) or friends.

During the coming week, contact each of these four people and ask if he or she wants to be at the biggest party in the whole world. You might visit the people on your list in person, call them on the phone, write them a letter, or send them a fax or E-mail message. You can explain to them that the biggest party in the world is the return of Jesus. Then ask them if they've accepted the free gift of eternal life. The decision they make will determine whether it will be the best party or the worst party they've ever been to in their whole lives. If they haven't accepted the free gift of eternal life, invite them to accept that gift from Jesus right now.

At our next lesson we'll share with each other the names of the persons we've invited to the party and what their responses were. I'll give you a few moments to write down their names. There are more than four lines, so you can keep adding names to the list.

(After the students have had time to write the names on their lists and ask questions of clarification, offer a closing prayer.)

SCRIPTURE SHEET 2
The Second Coming of Jesus

1. John 14:1-3:

What it means: _____

_____

2. 1 Thessalonians 4:16-18:

What it means: _____

_____

3. Revelation 20:1-10:

What it means: _____

_____

4. Matthew 24:14:

What it means: _____

_____

5. Matthew 28:19, 20:

What it means: _____

_____

WORK SHEET 2
The Second Coming of Jesus

1. What events will happen when Jesus comes the second time?

    a. _____

    b. _____

    c. _____

2. What events will happen during the millennium?

    a. _____

    b. _____

    c. _____

    d. _____

3. What events will happen when Jesus comes the *third* time?

    a. _____

    b. _____

    c. _____

    d. _____

    e. _____

FAMILY TALK BACK SHEET 2
The Second Coming of Jesus

1. What has been one of the "funnest" times in your life? Compare that event to the return of Jesus.

2. What would you like to do before Jesus returns (for example, get a driver's license, get married, visit Australia, etc.)?

3. A number of Christians believe that when Jesus comes He will secretly "rapture" His people to heaven. How would you respond to this belief? How would it affect the way you live?

4. Will you be glad or sad when Jesus returns? Why?

5. What do you think you'll do during the millennium?

6. Who do you want to be in heaven with you? What are you doing (and what have you done) to make this a reality?

7. Describe what you think heaven will be like. Why do you want to be there?

Baptismal Bible Study Guide Outline 3

CREATION AND THE SABBATH

Introduction: Follow up from study 2—party list *or* when is your birthday?

I. God created; if there's no God, we need another explanation (Genesis 1:1).
   A. The first verse in the Bible. Paraphrase of Genesis 1:1.
   B. God made the world (including you).
   C. The option of evolution.
   D. Do you believe in creation or evolution?

II. God created the Sabbath (Genesis 2:1-3).
   A. The events of Creation week.
   B. Sabbath as the birthday of the creation of our world (birthday cake).
   C. For Sabbath—rest, blessed, sanctified.

III. Jesus kept the Sabbath (Luke 4:16).
   A. Sabbath started with Creation.
   B. It continued with the Ten Commandments at Mount Sinai.
   C. Jesus kept the Sabbath too.
   D. Saturday is the Sabbath.
   E. Why do so many Christians worship on Sunday instead of on Sabbath?

IV. Don't stomp on the Sabbath; do God's things (Isaiah 58:13, 14).
   A. Doing your own pleasure.
   B. Doing God's things.

V. The Sabbath is for our good (Mark 2:27, 28).
   A. How the Sabbath can become a drag.
   B. God's intention for the Sabbath.
   C. What we can do.

VI. Conclusion: Your plans for making Sabbath special.

Baptismal Bible Study Guide 3

CREATION AND THE SABBATH

SCRIPTURE TEXTS:

1. Genesis 1:1: God created our world.
2. Genesis 2:1-3: God created the Sabbath.
3. Luke 4:16: Jesus kept the Sabbath.
4. Isaiah 58:13, 14: The Sabbath is a day to do God's kind of things.
5. Mark 2:27, 28: God made the Sabbath for our benefit.

DECISION TIME:

I believe God made the world—and me, too.

I want to keep the Sabbath holy by making specific plans to experience God's things this Sabbath.

MAKE IT CONCRETE (stage 3 appropriate):

Review what was made during each day of Creation week.

Have a birthday cake to celebrate the birthday of the world.

Note the cycles and their origin on a calendar.

Make a list of Sabbath activities and evaluate them.

MATERIALS NEEDED:

Basic study tools for each student—Bible, workbook Scripture Sheet 3, Work Sheet 3, pen or pencil.

Birthday cake with seven candles (bring plates, forks, and napkins).

INTRODUCTION:

(As a follow-up from study 2, have students report on the people they included on their invitation lists to the biggest party of all time—the second coming of Jesus.)

When is your birthday? Do you know the exact date, including the year, you were born? Write it down on Work Sheet 3.

What do you remember about being born?

(Field responses. Expect some silly answers.)

You may have seen a videotape of your birth, or maybe some photos, but nobody remembers what happened when he or she was born. We have to depend on what others have told us or shown us about the fact that we were born.

Some people are adopted, and sometimes it's not until they are teens or adults that they find out who their birth (biological) parents are. Some never find out who their parents are, and some don't have any record of the exact date they were born. Since we can't remember what happened when we were born, we believe the people we trust when they tell us the date we were born and who our parents are.

I. GENESIS 1:1: GOD CREATED OUR WORLD.

I know everyone can find our first text for today. It's the very first verse in the whole Bible—Genesis 1:1. Many of you probably know it by heart. Let's find out what it means.

(Have a student read it, then have everyone recite it as a group.)

What does that mean? Using your own words, somebody tell me what this verse is telling you.

(Have one or two volunteers share their understanding; then have each student write a paraphrase of the verse on Scripture Sheet 3.)

According to the Bible, God created everything. But who was there to see it? How many of you saw God create the world? Did anyone see God create the world? Right—nobody!

How many of you believe that God created the world?

(Ask for a showing of hands.)

And why do you believe that?

(Field responses. As you affirm the responses, accentuate the major items relevant to the discussion.)

Because we believe in God, and since we believe God has given us important messages in the Bible, it's easy to believe that God created the world—it's the very first message in the Bible! And if God created the world, who made you?

(Field responses. For those students who say their parents made them, ask: "Who made your parents?" If they start on the genealogy path, help them to see that it eventually goes back to the fact that we all go back to Adam, who was the son of God, according to Luke 3:37.)

Take a moment to think about that: you were made by God. That makes you a child of God. We have certain ideas of what other parents are like based on the kind of parents we have. But in a new sense, God is our parent. You may have a positive view of your parents. Or it might be a negative one. But God reminds us that while our parents may take care of us, especially when we're small, in a bigger sense God is the parent who will always take care of us.

But some people don't believe or trust God and the Bible. So when they hear that God made them, they don't believe it. How unfortunate that they refuse to accept the fact that they are children of God! When you ask them "Who made you?" they will answer "My parents." But if you ask them to trace their family tree back to its start, they won't end up with God being the original parent. Instead, they give the story of evolution. They'll explain that millions of years ago our ancestors were monkeys, not people. And before that, they were sea creatures. Just as nobody alive today saw God create our world, nobody saw sea animals crawl out onto the land and eventually turn into monkeys and finally become people.

So which story would you rather believe? Both stories have some evidence, but nobody living today saw either one happen. Which story you believe comes down to a matter of whether you believe God and the Bible or not. Let's look at questions 2 and 3 on our Work Sheet.

(Help students respond in writing to the questions of who made them.)

Who made you? I suppose it depends on whether or not you believe in God. Let me ask you this: Would you rather believe you are a child of God, or a child of a monkey or sea animal, or slime mold? I believe in God, so I believe I'm a child of God. How about you?

II. GENESIS 2:1-3: GOD CREATED THE SABBATH.

As a review, let's identify what God made on the different days of Creation week. Instead of taking millions of years to mutate our world into existence, God chose to create it in one week. He could have done the whole thing in an instant (after all, He is God!), but He decided on seven days instead. Why seven days? We probably won't know until we ask Him in heaven. But that's what He decided. If we can't quite remember what was created each day, we can look in the first chapter of the Bible. It's already been written there for our instruction and review.

First day: light (verses 3-5).

Second day: air (verses 6-8).

Third day: land, plants, flowers, trees (verses 9-13).

Fourth day: sun, moon, and stars (verses 14-19).

Fifth day: fish and other sea animals, birds (verses 20-23).

Sixth day: animals (on land) and humans (verses 24-27).

Seventh day: Sabbath (Genesis 2:2, 3).

Let's read about God's creation of the Sabbath. It comes at the end of the Creation story, in Genesis 2:1-3.

(Have a student read the passage aloud. Then have another student offer a paraphrase. After some discussion, students can write their own paraphrases on their Scripture Sheets.)

The Sabbath is the birthday for the Creation of our world. God set it up as a "day of rest" so He could celebrate His Creation. When we celebrate the Sabbath we demonstrate our belief that God created the world, and are reminded that we are His children. That can be very helpful when you feel like a failure because you recently flunked a test, or you feel like a reject because people have been talking behind your back, or a friend isn't being a friend anymore. It can help when you don't live up to your expectations for yourself or what your parents or teachers expect of you. Each week the Sabbath can remind us that no matter what happens or has happened, we are children of God because He made us!

Maybe it would be a good idea to be reminded of that each Sabbath. Even if you don't have a birthday cake and candles, at least use your imagination to remember that you're celebrating the birthday of the world.

(At this time bring out a birthday cake with seven candles, or a candle in the shape of the number 7. Sing "Happy Birthday" to the world and have someone blow out the candles. Point out that with the birthday of the world, we acknowledge God as our Creator and that we are part of His creation. This has implications for our identity and our relationship to the rest of creation.)

Besides the fact that God created the Sabbath, Genesis 2:1-3 gives us a clue

44

about the Sabbath. Consider these three words: "rest," "blessed," "sanctified" (made holy).

We sometimes think of the word "rest" as only meaning sleep. Actually, the word means *stop!* It's what God did on the Sabbath. He wasn't taking a snooze because He was behind on His sleep—He stopped because He had finished creating the entire world. It was time to take a break from everything He had been doing. In the same way, the Sabbath is a day for us to *stop* what we have been doing all week. What are some things you do during the week that would be worth stopping on Sabbath?

(Field responses from students and feel free to comment.)

Our passage also mentions that God "blessed" the Sabbath. We don't use that word very often, but basically it means to be happy. In other words, the Sabbath is a day for happiness and joy. This doesn't just automatically happen; it comes as a result of doing certain things and not doing certain other things. You can't just be happy. You can't just force it on somebody. It's a result (or by-product) of choices and events.

What has made you happy? The Sabbath is especially a day for participation in joyous activities. Because you've stopped what you do on other days of the week, you're able to pursue these other important experiences. You'll probably need to make some plans in advance to do some of these things. What are some things you have done or could do to make the Sabbath "blessed"?

(Field responses from students and be prepared to share some of your own. Keep in mind that what makes you happy won't necessarily make a young person happy. They usually prefer lively, on-the-go activities.)

The third word from our text is "sanctified," or made holy. Perhaps we can better understand this word if we think of saving something special. For instance, when it comes to clothing, we may save a new special outfit for an important occasion, such as the first social gathering of the school year; or we might get a new pair of cleats for a big football or baseball game. If we have a good photo of ourselves, we may save it to give to someone who is special to us, and on the back of the photo we may write a personal message that we wouldn't write to just anybody. When something is sanctified, it's special.

When it comes to the Sabbath being sanctified, we mean having special things saved just for Sabbath. Some people have special meals; perhaps cinnamon rolls for Sabbath breakfast and a special lunch with the entire family. Some reserve special family outings at the beach, the mountains, a lake, a cave, or some other place especially for Sabbath. Some have "Sabbath clothes" that they wear only on Sabbath.

God sanctified the Sabbath, which means He has saved it as a special time. We receive benefits when we follow the same process of saving/planning things especially for Sabbath. While God is available to us every day, we don't always make time for God on a daily basis. The Sabbath is an ideal time saved for focused time with God. After all, on Sabbath we have stopped what we usually do during the week, so we have time for the special things we've saved for Sabbath.

III. LUKE 4:16: JESUS KEPT THE SABBATH.

Some people think the seventh-day Sabbath is just for the Jews. They think the

Sabbath started on Mount Sinai with the giving of the Ten Commandments to the Jews. The fourth commandment (Exodus 20:8-11) told the Jews to remember the Sabbath day to keep it holy. God gave us the Sabbath as something special. When we "keep" the Sabbath holy, we make it special, just as God intended. Evidently, the Jews had forgotten to keep the Sabbath holy, because in this text God told them to "remember" it.

But it wasn't just because they probably didn't keep the Sabbath holy while they were slaves in Egypt—the Sabbath had its beginning at Creation—remember? In fact, right in the fourth commandment we are told the reason to keep it holy—not because we're Jews, but because God created the world in six days and rested on the seventh day. The Sabbath is the birthday of the creation of our world. It's for everyone on the earth, not just the Jews. The counsel to "remember the Sabbath day to keep it holy" is for us, too.

In fact, when Jesus became a human being 2,000 years ago, He kept the Sabbath too. Let's turn to Luke 4:16 and read about it.

(Have one student read the passage and have others paraphrase after discussing it. Students can write their own paraphrases on their Scripture Sheets.)

The major emphasis of the whole passage in this part of Luke is that Jesus was the Messiah and He was rejected in His hometown. The fact that He went to the synagogue, or church, on Sabbath as He always did, is just the lead-up to the amazing incident.

Can you believe that Jesus was rejected by people at church on Sabbath? Evidently, going to church on Sabbath isn't a guarantee that you have it all together. But *not* going to church or keeping the Sabbath holy because some religious people blow it is a lame excuse for *you* to not go to church or keep the Sabbath holy. Jesus, who was perfect, kept the Sabbath. He is our example in Sabbathkeeping, too.

Some people wonder if Saturday is really the Sabbath. Let's take a look at a typical calendar.

(Have a one-year calendar that's divided into months and shows the days of the week. It would be good to also have a "business calendar" that shows Monday as the first [business] day of the week.)

Help me to understand which day is the seventh day on the calendar.

(Show students the calendar.)

Is this too obvious? Am I missing something here? Is Thursday the seventh day of the week?

Now, some people have come up with another type of calendar that has Monday as the first day of the week. They do this for people in business who make appointments on Monday through Friday and then take off for the weekend. Their workweek begins on Monday, so special calendars have been made for them that have Monday first, which makes Sunday the seventh day.

(Show a copy of a business calendar that has Monday as the first day of the week.)

But if you ask even people in business, they will tell you that the first day of the week is Sunday and the seventh day is Saturday. And while the Sabbath isn't just for Jews, the Jews have kept careful records of the days of the week for thousands of years. The seventh day is still the seventh day—Saturday equals Sabbath!

We can also look at this from a scientific point of view. Our calendar is based on movements within our solar system. How long does it take for the earth to make one complete rotation on its axis?

(Allow students to respond.)

That's right, one day—approximately 24 hours. And how long does it take for the earth to rotate around the sun?

(Allow students to answer.)

Correct—one year. Then what happens during the time period we call a month?

(Once again, let the students respond. Fewer are likely to know that the monthly cycle is derived from the time it takes the moon to rotate around the earth.)

That's why each month there is a "new moon."

As you can see, our calendars are divided into segments based on various movements within our solar system. The other time segment on the calendar is the week. What happens during the time period we call a week?

(Let the students respond. There is no known event in our solar system based on the weekly cycle.)

Our week is based on the creation of our world. Isn't it amazing that all of us operate on a weekly cycle—even people who don't believe God created our world or that the seventh day is the Sabbath!

This brings up a logical question about people who do believe God created the world, but who don't keep the seventh day as the Sabbath. Let me phrase it this way: Why do so many Christians go to church on Sunday instead of on Sabbath? What have you heard, or what would you guess?

(Field responses from students.)

Surprisingly, most of the people who go to church on Sunday think the Bible says that Sunday is the day of worship. Few even question whether or not the Bible says a different day of the week is the Sabbath. When pressed, they will give such reasons as "Jesus was resurrected on Sunday, so we go to church on Sunday in memory of the Resurrection." It's a good idea to celebrate the Resurrection every Easter; but that's once a year, not once a week! Some will even say that it doesn't matter which day of the week you keep holy, as long as you do it sometime.

When people try to show from the Bible that Sunday is the Sabbath, they're at a real disadvantage, because the Bible never makes such a statement. In fact, Christians didn't start worshiping on Sunday until after the Bible was completed. No wonder the Bible doesn't say anything about it. One reason Christians started worshiping on Sunday was to be different from the Jews, who already worshiped on Sabbath. However, when it comes to making any day but the seventh day the Sabbath, it's a matter of going with what God made clear in the Bible, or else substituting humanity's ideas in place of God's. A majority of Christians making Sunday their Sabbath for hundreds of years doesn't make it right. Who said the majority is always right? And keeping the seventh day of the week as the Sabbath goes back even before the Bible was written—to the creation of our world! No wonder we have the record of the seventh-day Sabbath in the Bible.

If you were born on January 28, 1986, then that's the day to celebrate your birthday. Sometimes we actually celebrate our birthdays a few days before or after the actual date, if that's more convenient for family members and friends. But that doesn't change the date we were born. You certainly wouldn't celebrate your birthday in July if you were born in January! So why should we celebrate the Sabbath on Sunday?

IV. ISAIAH 58:13, 14: THE SABBATH IS A DAY TO DO GOD'S KIND OF THINGS.

It's one thing to say that the seventh day is the Sabbath. It's another thing to experience everything God intended for us on this special day. We've already noted that three key words for keeping the Sabbath are "rest," "blessed," and "sanctified." Another way of looking at this special day can be found in Isaiah 58:13, 14.

(Have one student read it; then open the floor for discussion about what the text means. Following the discussion, have students write their own paraphrase on their Scripture Sheets.)

Some people get the idea from this text that if anything is pleasurable—that "doing your own pleasure" equals fun—it must be wrong for Sabbath. But the very next phrase talks about calling the Sabbath a delight. The difference is whether you're doing things from your perspective or from God's perspective. We could paraphrase this verse by saying, "Stop doing your own thing on God's Sabbath. Instead, do the kinds of things God knows would make you happy."

What are some of those things? Do items 4 and 5 on Work Sheet 3 and brainstorm to come up with some ideas. And don't forget the three principles of "rest," "blessed," and "sanctified."

(Refer to items 4 and 5 on Work Sheet 3.)

V. MARK 2:27, 28: GOD MADE THE SABBATH FOR OUR BENEFIT.

Perhaps you've experienced some Sabbaths that weren't anywhere close to what God intended. Sometimes people make lots of rules for what to do and what not to do on Sabbath—to the point that Sabbath becomes the worst day of the week. That's what Sabbath had become when Jesus was on earth. Sometimes we make it just as bad, even though we may have great intentions for making the Sabbath special.

Let's not forget what Jesus said when people accused Him of breaking the Sabbath. You can read it in Mark 2:27.

(Have one student read the text and let each person write a paraphrase of it on Scripture Sheet 3.)

God didn't create us to keep the Sabbath. God created the Sabbath for our benefit—to celebrate the creation of our world, to remind us that we are His children, and to give us time to get reoriented every week to His perspective.

CONCLUSION:

As a child of God, part of His creation, do you desire to experience God's orientation to things by focusing on God's perspective this Sabbath? If you do, what specific plans will you make for this to become a reality?

SCRIPTURE SHEET 3
Creation and the Sabbath

1. Genesis 1:1:

What it means: _____

_____

2. Genesis 2:1-3:

What it means: _____

_____

3. Luke 4:16:

What it means: _____

_____

4. Isaiah 58:13, 14:

What it means: _____

_____

5. Mark 2:27, 28:

What it means: _____

_____

WORK SHEET 3
Creation and the Sabbath

1. **When were you born?** _____ _____ _____
   month   day   year

2. **If there is a God, who made you?** _____

3. **If there is no God, who made you?** _____

4. **Why do so many Christians go to church on Sunday instead of on Sabbath?**

   _____

   _____

   _____

5. **Put an X by the activities you think would be good to do on Sabbath:**
   - ○ Go shopping
   - ○ Go hiking
   - ○ Clean the house
   - ○ Watch TV
   - ○ Visit people in the hospital
   - ○ Go to Sabbath school and church
   - ○ Help at a soup kitchen
   - ○ Do things with your family

6. **What activities do you like to do on Sabbath?**

   _____

   _____

FAMILY TALK BACK SHEET 3
Creation and the Sabbath

1. Do you find it easier to believe in creation or in evolution? Why?

2. What do you think of when you hear the word "Sabbath"?

3. What Sabbath traditions do you have in your family? What Sabbath traditions would you like to have?

4. Why do you worship on Sabbath? Does it really make any difference as long as you choose one day a week for worship? Explain.

5. When people ask you why you go to church on Saturday instead of on Sunday, what explanation do you give?

6. Describe one of the best Sabbaths you can remember.

7. What part do you play in making the Sabbath a delight?

Baptismal Bible Study Guide Outline 4

STANDARDS

Introduction: Owner's manual for a piece of equipment, such as a computer.

I. Everything belongs to God/Jesus (Romans 12:1-3).
   A. As babies we're under our parents' control.
   B. As we grow up we develop self-control.
   C. It's up to you to choose whether or not to follow God.
   D. As far as you're concerned, does "everything belong to God"?

II. The Sabbath is one seventh of our time (Exodus 20:8-11).
   A. One day out of the seven-day week.
   B. How much of our time belongs to God—one day or seven days?

III. Tithe is one tenth of our income; we give it at church (Malachi 3:10).
   A. One tenth = tithe.
   B. Mathematical problems for determining one tenth.
   C. The church is the storehouse mentioned in Malachi 3:10.
   D. How is the tithe used?
   E. How do you spend the other nine tenths?

IV. Things of the world versus the things of God (1 John 2:15-17).
   A. The things of the world.
   B. The things of God.

V. Our bodies belong to God (1 Corinthians 6:19, 20).
   A. "It's *my* body." Really?
   B. Healthful living, because our bodies belong to God.
   C. NEWSTART.
   D. Commonsense rules for taking care of new equipment.

VI. Conclusion: As far as you're concerned, does everything belong to God? If not, why not? If so, what specific things will you do or not do to live this way?

Baptismal Bible Study Guide 4

STANDARDS

SCRIPTURE TEXTS:
1. Romans 12:1-3: Everything belongs to God/Jesus.
2. Exodus 20:8-11: The Sabbath is one seventh of our time.
3. Malachi 3:10: Tithe is one tenth of our income; we give it at church.
4. 1 John 2:15-17: Things of the world versus the things of God.
5. 1 Corinthians 6:19, 20: Our bodies belong to God.

DECISION TIME:
Dedicate or rededicate oneself to God 100 percent in a willingness to follow God's specific instructions regarding how we live for Him.

MAKE IT CONCRETE (stage 3 appropriate):
Figure out how much tithe a person would pay on various amounts of money.
Identify specific things that are worldly and specific things that are godly.
Identify health rules based on the acronym NEWSTART.
Make a set of rules for sports equipment.

MATERIALS NEEDED:
Basic study tools for each student—Bible, workbook Scripture Sheet 4, workbook Work Sheet 4, pen or pencil.
Instruction booklet(s) for sophisticated equipment.
Whiteboard or flipchart and markers.
New sports equipment.

INTRODUCTION:
When a person buys a new computer or other piece of sophisticated equipment, there are extensive instructions included on how to operate it.

(Show a booklet of instructions on setting up and operating a computer or other equipment.)

Some people carefully follow every step given in the instructions, even though it takes quite awhile. Others don't follow the instructions at all, but try to figure things out on their own. And many people do a little of both—following some of the instructions, then figuring other things out on their own, then returning to the instructions when they get stuck. How closely would you follow the instructions that come with a new computer?

I. ROMANS 12:1-3: EVERYTHING BELONGS TO GOD/JESUS.
In the process of growing up, you eventually begin to realize that your parents

53

don't completely control you. In fact, at this point in your life your parents hope that you have lots of "self-control." They may be interested in what you do and don't do, but they want you to make your own choices. As you know, you get to experience the consequences of those choices. You learn which consequences are good and which ones you'd rather not have again. That's part of reaching maturity.

Making a decision to be baptized is another example of being able to choose for yourself. If you were a baby—or even 5 years old—and got baptized, it would be because your parents chose that for you. But your decision to be baptized now needs to be *your* decision, regardless if some people want you to do it or don't want you to do it.

As they make more and more of their own choices, some young people get the idea that their independence from their parents makes them independent from everyone and everything. But even adults are not independent of the rules in our society. Can you run stoplights just because you're an adult? Is it OK to drive while you're drunk, as long as you're not a teenager? Of course not! Even "independent" people have rules to follow. And this is true also of how we relate to people socially. When adults gossip about other people, there are hurt feelings and petty fights, just like with kids.

When you were a child, your parents instructed you on how to live. Their experience enabled them to teach you things it would have taken you a long time to learn on your own. Most parents readily admit that they've made some mistakes in their parenting, but they have also done quite a few things right.

Now you're to the point that God is replacing your parents as the one who can teach you things it would take you a lot longer to learn on your own. Some of your peers will choose to live without God, and they will learn a lot of things "the hard way." Actually, your independence gives you the freedom to choose whether or not you want to live by God's guidance.

For those who choose to follow God, it's a *huge* choice. That's because God asks us to give Him *everything* when we follow Him. It's not a decision to be taken lightly. Are you ready and willing to give God everything? Your friends, your music, your abilities, your clothes, your time, your reputation, your money, your body—everything?

Some things are pretty hard to give up. If friends are very important to you, it's hard to give them up. If you don't like your body, it's pretty easy to give that to God. But God asks for absolutely everything. That's because He has given us everything. We can read about it in Romans 12:1-3.

In the first part of the book of Romans, Paul explains that everyone is a sinner and is lost. But Jesus came and died for us so that we can be forgiven and live forever with Him. This offer is available if we choose to trust Jesus for this incredible gift. That's the background to Romans 12.

(Have one student read the passage, then have other students explain what it means to them. Following the discussion, students can write their own paraphrase of the passage on Scripture Sheet 4.)

Take a look at the first question on Work Sheet 4: "How much of ourselves belongs to God?" This seems like a simple question, but it makes a big difference in how you relate to everything.

(Allow students to respond to the question.)

While it's true that everything belongs to God, not everyone acknowledges that fact. When you believe that everything belongs to God, you're open to accepting and living by what God says instead of ignoring it or going against it. You believe what God says because you realize that He knows what He's talking about.

II. EXODUS 20:8-11: THE SABBATH IS ONE SEVENTH OF OUR TIME.

In our last study we talked about the Sabbath. Let's review it as it is found in the Ten Commandments. Turn to Exodus 20:8-11.

(Have students find the passage and have one person read it. Then have everyone try reciting it in unison—probably the KJV. Ask them what these verses mean in light of how we live when we realize that everything, including our time, belongs to God. Then students can write their own paraphrase of this passage on Scripture Sheet 4.)

Some Seventh-day Adventists have the idea that the Sabbath belongs to God and the rest of the week belongs to them. How can that be? It seems that such people treat their time with God like bad-tasting medicine. They don't like it, but it probably will help them some. Once they've had their medicine, they can go back to doing what they want—completely apart from God!

Those who follow Christ realize that everything, including *all* of our time, belongs to God. That includes more than just the Sabbath. Who would want to limit their time with God to just the Sabbath hours of the week?

Think of it this way: You might get to spend time hanging out with friends on the weekend. Does that mean you'll never want to talk to those friends during the week? If you see them at school, will you avoid them, since you already saw them on the weekend? Will you refuse to talk to them on the phone because you already talked to them at Sabbath school? Of course not! That's ridiculous! Perhaps we need to think of God as our friend, instead of as a mean police officer.

III. MALACHI 3:10: TITHE IS ONE TENTH OF OUR INCOME. WE RETURN IT TO GOD AT CHURCH.

We've been talking about our time, but what about our money? First of all, let's remember our starting point—everything belongs to God. We may refer to it as *our* money, but we recognize that as Christians we have given everything to God. He doesn't snatch away the few dollars we have, but now we use the money in our possession the way God would want it to be used.

How does God want the money to be used? Let's find out part of the answer in Malachi 3:10.

(Have one student read it. Let others comment on the passage. Then have students write their paraphrases of this verse on Scripture Sheet 4.)

Tithe is one tenth. If that's true, let's do a little bit of math on our Work Sheets. *(Have students write in the answers to question 3 on Work Sheet 4.)*

Figuring out the tithe is simply a matter of moving the decimal point one digit to the left. Round off the number, if need be—do you remember your rounding-off rules? This is a good time to go beyond the "letter" of the law to the "spirit" of the law. How much difference does it really make if we have $2.48 or $2.47 left after returning tithe on $2.75?

Returning tithe when we first receive money helps to remind us that *all* of our money belongs to God. Do you trust that God will be able to take care of you with the remaining nine tenths of the money, or do you have the misconception that you're really on your own?

Our text in Malachi says to take the tithe to the storehouse. Where is the storehouse? Most of us aren't farmers, so we don't take one tenth of our harvested corn or carrots to a storehouse. We take our tithe to the church to return it to God. The tithe is used to pay for the pastors in our churches so they can serve as ministers on a full-time basis.

The tithe doesn't pay for the electricity or church bulletins or community service. People give offerings *in addition* to their tithe because they believe God wants them to support these things. This isn't *in place* of returning the one tenth to God's storehouse; this is *in addition* to it. And many people say they receive a blessing by giving more.

Have you tried it? How would God want you to spend the remaining nine tenths after you return your tithe to God?

IV. 1 JOHN 2:15-17: WE CHOOSE BETWEEN THE THINGS OF THIS WORLD AND THE THINGS OF GOD.

Time and money are very specific. But even with these, God gives us lots of variety in how we will spend the majority of time and the majority of the money He's given us. So how can we know how to spend these things in the way God would want us to? God gave His followers a commonsense answer to that question. It's found in 1 John 2:15-17.

(Have one student read the passage, then open it up for discussion. Then have students write their own paraphrases of these verses on their Scripture Sheet 4.)

That's pretty basic—dividing everything into two categories: the things of this world, and the things of God. Because your heart always follows the things you invest in with your time and money (Matthew 6:21), you can shape your affections either toward the world or toward God, based upon how you spend your time and money.

Item 4 on your Work Sheet gives two blank lists for you to fill out. The list on the left is the things of the world. The other list is the things of God. Take some time now to write what could go on each of these lists.

(This is an ideal time for students to begin to differentiate between specific behaviors and what's behind those behaviors. It's also a great time to discuss associations that accompany various behaviors. Most students will be able to begin to internalize things their parents and others have been trying to teach them for years.)

V. 1 CORINTHIANS 6:19, 20: OUR BODIES BELONG TO GOD.

In the 1960s some hippies became very interested in healthful living. The motivation was to have a healthy body that would give them a better high when they took their drugs. What an interesting concept—take care of your body so you can get more out of destroying it!

One of the arguments used when people debate the issue of abortion is that a woman's body belongs to her, versus the unborn's body belonging to the unborn. Neither argument is correct, according to the Bible. We can discover who "owns" our bodies by reading 1 Corinthians 6:19, 20.

(Have one student read the passage, followed by all students writing a para-phrase of these verses on their Scripture Sheet 4.)

To whom do our bodies belong? Some people will deny it until they die, but God created us, died for us, and will return and give us a new body. In the meantime our bodies belong to God. Christians readily recognize this.

But the verses we read were directed to Christians who said that since their minds belonged to God they could do whatever they wanted with their bodies. Some of them decided to have sex with prostitutes. They reasoned, "My body belongs to me, so I can do whatever I want with it." Paul told them, "Absolutely not!" Our bodies belong to God. Besides, what we do with our bodies affects our emotions, our minds, and even our spiritual perceptions.

No wonder Seventh-day Adventists are so interested in healthful living. How we live affects other parts of our lives, too. And even though we have bodies that are quite inferior to the ones God created in the Garden of Eden, how we care for the bodies we have makes a difference. This doesn't mean that all of us can eat our way to the perfect body, or even exercise to a bodybuilder's physique. But we do have several guidelines for healthful living. One way to remember these keys is the acronym NEWSTART.

(Refer to Work Sheet 4, item 5).

N stands for *nutrition.* This has to do with our diet. Some people may be vegetarians, but they eat loads of sugary desserts. And some people eat lots of fruit, but rarely eat any vegetables. Others stuff themselves with empty calories by eating junk food between meals all the time. The basic concept of good nutrition is to eat the best food available. Usually, the results of our eating habits show up over a long period of time. Overeating once won't make a person obese; doing it on a regular basis will. What habits have you already developed? Which ones would you like to have?

E is for *exercise.* Because so many of us spend most of the day not using much physical energy, we need to exercise intentionally. A physical education class might give us that opportunity. Some people jog or ride a bike. Others belong to health clubs. Working in the yard or taking a brisk walk can provide great exercise. What types of exercise do you get each week?

W is for *water.* The standard rule continues to be "eight glasses a day." In some climates your body requires even more. Think of it in terms of washing a sheet. Is it easier to clean a sheet with a cup of water or with five gallons of water? The inside of your body needs lots of water to do its job. And don't neglect washing the outside, either!

S is for *sunshine.* Sunshine helps our bodies produce vitamin D, and some people believe that getting sunshine improves their attitude as well. This doesn't mean the more sun you get, the better you will feel. If you've had a sunburn, you know what it's like to get too much of a good thing! Which brings us to the next letter.

T is for *temperance.* This concept has two parts to it. The first is to stay away from everything bad—smoking, for example. Although some do it to be "fashionable" and others do it to be defiant, smoking is basically very bad for our bodies. The second component of temperance is moderation in even things that are good for you—like sunshine. Although water is good for us, that doesn't mean we should drink 10 gallons every day. Moderation—a healthy amount—is part of temperance.

A is for *air.* Of course, we need air just to survive. Breathing is one way our bodies take in good elements and eliminate bad ones. Exercise, especially intense exercise, helps us to breathe deeply. Some areas have such severe air pollution that getting fresh air is a problem. Air is another important principle for healthy living.

R is for *rest.* At first people will think this is about getting enough sleep. That's certainly part of it. Most people need seven to eight hours of sleep each night. During adolescence there may be times when you need more because of growth spurts. But rest also has to do with having a change of pace. That was the first principle for keeping Sabbath holy—to stop what we've been doing all week and rest.

T is for *trust in God.* God not only created us; He also keeps us going. When we trust Him we receive peace of mind, which has a positive impact on our emotional and physical well-being. What a relief to have our anxieties taken away by trusting in God!

Because most of these principles make their biggest difference over a long period of time, it's usually older people who are most concerned about them. Young people rarely have an interest in healthful living, because getting old seems so far away. Ironically, it's the habits you follow now that will determine the quantity and quality of your life for years to come. These guidelines aren't meant to make life miserable. They're for just the opposite purpose—to make life better.

It's like rules you might establish for taking care of new sports equipment.

(If you have new sports equipment to show the group, it would make this illustration much more realistic and powerful.)

What rules would you recommend for making sure this equipment stays in good condition and lasts a reasonable period of time?

(Field responses. You may need to offer some suggestions, such as "Have people check out equipment and be responsible for returning it," and "Use equipment for its intended use—don't use volleyballs as kickballs, or use the minitrampoline for high jumping.)

CONCLUSION:

Our starting point for this Bible study was that everything belongs to God. That means us, our time, our money, our bodies—everything. But we have a choice regarding whether or not we will acknowledge this fact and live by it.

Today I'd like you to decide if you want to give yourself 100 percent to God. You may have done this in the past, or this might be the first time. If your decision is yes, then I'd like you to share with us just one of the specific things you'll choose to do as you live for God.

(Give students some time to think about this choice and then to verbalize it. If they need help identifying specific behaviors, direct them back to their own Work Sheets. Be ready to give lots of affirmation as they identify ways to personally live for God. Close with prayer.)

SCRIPTURE SHEET 4
Standards

1. Romans 12:1-3:

What it means: _____

_____

2. Exodus 20:8-11:

What it means: _____

_____

3. Malachi 3:10:

What it means: _____

_____

4. 1 John 2:15-17:

What it means: _____

_____

5. 1 Corinthians 6:19, 20:

What it means: _____

_____

WORK SHEET 4
Standards

1. How much of ourselves belongs to God? _____

2. How much of our time belongs to God? _____

   The Sabbath is how much of our time? _____

3. How much of our money is a tithe? _____

   How much tithe would you return if you earned $1.00? _____

   How much tithe would you return if you earned $2.75? _____

4. List some "things of the world."   List some "things of God."

   _____   _____

   _____   _____

   _____   _____

5. What does NEWSTART stand for?

   N _____   S _____

   E _____   T _____

   W _____   A _____

                                   R _____

                                   T _____

FAMILY TALK BACK SHEET 4
Standards

1. Does everything you have belong to God? Why, or why not?

2. Make a list of the things you buy and how much of your income (or what percentage) is spent on those items. How does this relate to "Where your treasure is, there will your heart be also" (Matthew 6:21)?

3. How often does our family have "family time" together? Do you wish we had more time or less time together? What does it take for you to have enough time to be with friends? What does it take for you to have enough time to be with God?

4. What "things of the world" are a temptation to you—possessions, clothing, popularity, fun times, experimentation, alcohol, sex, selfishness, music, rebellion? Which items are not much of a temptation for you at this time?

5. Whom does your body belong to—yourself, your parents, God, a boyfriend or girlfriend? What difference does that make?

6. What habit patterns do you have for healthy living, such as diet, sleep, exercise, good air and water, self-control, moderation, etc.?

7. Who determines what your personal standards will be? What does it take for you to change your standards? What does it take for you to keep them?

Baptismal Bible Study Guide Outline 5

SYMBOLS

Introduction: Olympic gold medals and other symbols, such as a flag.

  I.   Baptism is the symbol for the forgiveness of sins (Mark 1:4).
       A. Other symbols.
       B. Revised pictionary.
       C. Baptism is the symbol for forgiveness.

 II.   Repent; baptism for forgiveness; receive the Holy Spirit (Acts 2:38).
       A. Read and paraphrase Acts 2:38.
       B. Repentance precedes baptism.
       C. Baptism can also symbolize that the Holy Spirit enters a person's life.

III.   The first foot washing; example of Jesus (John 13:10, 14, 15).
       A. Background for the symbol of foot washing.
       B. Why we do it today.

 IV.   Symbol of the bread (1 Corinthians 11:23, 24).
       A. The first Lord's Supper and the change from the Passover.
       B. The bread symbolizes our basic needs—Jesus cares for these.

  V.   Symbol of the grape juice; "till He comes" (1 Corinthians 11:25, 26).
       A. Grape juice symbolizes the blood of Jesus.
       B. Also contains the promise of His return.

 VI: Conclusion: What the symbol of baptism means to you and an invitation for you to choose to be baptized if you want the symbol to be the reality in your life.

Baptismal Bible Study Guide 5

SYMBOLS

SCRIPTURE TEXTS:

1. Mark 1:4: Baptism is the symbol for the forgiveness of sins.
2. Acts 2:38: Repent; baptism for forgiveness; receive the Holy Spirit.
3. John 13:10, 14, 15: The first foot washing; example of Jesus.
4. 1 Corinthians 11:23, 24: Symbol of the bread.
5. 1 Corinthians 11:25, 26: Symbol of the grape juice; till He comes.

DECISION TIME:

Write down what baptism means to me.

I choose to be baptized.

I choose to participate fully in the symbols of the church, namely, baptism, foot washing, and the Lord's Supper.

MAKE IT CONCRETE (stage 3 appropriate):

Show recognizable symbols.

Have participants draw and guess symbols.

Demonstrate the victory/peace symbol of two fingers raised.

Foot-washing basins and towels.

Bread and grape juice from the Lord's Supper.

MATERIALS NEEDED:

Basic study tools for each student—Bible, workbook Scripture Sheet 5, workbook Work Sheet 4, pen or pencil.

Collection of symbolic markings, such as logos, etc.

Flipchart or whiteboard, markers, and pens.

Foot-washing basins and towels.

Bread and grape juice for the Lord's Supper.

INTRODUCTION:

When Olympic athletes win a gold medal, they have a symbol they will treasure forever. That medal, which is gold only on the cover, represents something far more than just a piece of metal. It stands for all the practice that led to the Olympics. It includes all the competitions the athlete had to pass through just to qualify to participate in the Olympics. It symbolizes that the person is a winner.

And when the medal is awarded, the national anthem is played as the flag is raised—both symbols of the athlete's country. A flag is not a country, but at that moment it symbolizes the country. It's a recognition that the athlete is part of a bigger picture, just one person in an entire country that shares this moment of glory. In a sense, the athlete is a symbol of the country, since he or she represents that country.

I. MARK 1:4: BAPTISM IS THE SYMBOL FOR THE FORGIVENESS OF SINS.

We use symbols all the time. People attending a funeral are likely to wear the color black to symbolize their sorrow. A flag will be flown at half-mast when a national figure dies. Many married people wear a wedding ring to symbolize their marriage. The wedding ring is not what makes them married; it symbolizes their commitment to each other.

There are lots of ways to say "I love you" besides just using the words. Some people give roses, and others sing songs. How else do people say "I love you"?

(Have students offer some responses.)

And what are some other symbols we use, such as shaking hands for a greeting or giving a high five for congratulations?

(Field responses from students. You may need to give a few more examples until they get the hang of it. Write the word car *on a whiteboard or flipchart, then ask what it is. When they respond with the word "car," become extremely literalistic and explain that it is not really a car, but just lines of ink on paper. They may be perplexed at first, but continue your explanation.)*

Even the words we spell are symbols. You cannot take the word "car" and drive it down the street. The letters symbolize a machine we know as a car. In fact, even the letters themselves are symbols. The letter *C* is simply an incomplete circle, but we have given it the meaning of a letter in our alphabet. And that symbol can mean either a *k* sound as in *cat,* or an *s* sound, as in *center.*

You've probably played some form of the game of Pictionary, in which people draw symbols and you guess what they are—literally. For example, if we were guessing Bible names and I drew a picture of a shepherd's crook *(draw a shepherd's crook on the board),* you'd probably guess Cain, because another name for a walking stick is a cane, and Cain is a Bible name.

But we're going to play the game a little differently today. Instead of saying what the drawing is literally, think of what the drawing could represent. For example, if we were still thinking of Bible names and I drew a shepherd's crook, you might think of Moses or David, who were famous shepherds. Or you might think of Jesus, who was known as the Good Shepherd.

I'll draw a few symbols for you to guess, then you try some.

(You can use the blanks at the top of Work Sheet 5, or let students respond out loud. Draw familiar logos, such as the golden arches [McDonald's], a polo player [Ralph Lauren polo shirt insignia], an American flag, a star of David, an apple with a bite out of it [Apple computer], the letters SDA, a cross, a heart, a swastika, the math symbol for division, a logo for a local business, etc. Once students get the idea, encourage a few of them to try drawing symbols that the others will understand.)

God has given us symbols too. One of them is found in Mark 1:4. Tell me what you think the symbol is and what it represents.

(Have a student read the passage and let others identify the symbol and tell what it represents. Then have students record their paraphrases on their Scripture Sheet 5. This can be followed by doing question 2 on Work Sheet 5. Please note that there can be more than one correct answer. Let this spark additional discussion.)

To represent having one's sins completely washed away (forgiven), John the Baptist used the symbol of allowing oneself to be completely lowered under the water. I suppose he could have used soap and a washcloth just as well, but he chose immersion as the symbol for forgiveness. It's no wonder that John balked at baptizing Jesus and suggested that, rather, Jesus should baptize *him* (Matthew 3:13-15). Jesus had no sins to be washed away, but even John the Baptist did. Yet Jesus gave us an example of being baptized.

Have you ever sinned? I have. Going under the water doesn't literally wash away your sins. People do it to symbolize that they have asked Jesus to forgive them of all their sins. Have you asked Jesus to forgive you of all your sins? Have you experienced the symbol of this forgiveness by being baptized? Many of you will be baptized at the end of these Bible studies. You will then have experienced the symbol of complete forgiveness of sins.

II. ACTS 2:38: REPENTANCE PRECEDES BAPTISM. BAPTISM SYMBOLIZES THE FORGIVENESS OF SINS AND THE RECEPTION OF THE HOLY SPIRIT.

It's one thing to go swimming and get dunked under the water; it's quite another thing to truly experience baptism. Let's read about it in Acts 2:38. The setting for this verse is Peter's sermon, just after Jesus had been crucified and resurrected, and had returned to heaven. The disciples, filled with the Holy Spirit, were boldly sharing the story of Jesus. After hearing Peter's powerful sermon, his listeners felt convicted to respond to the message. Here's what Peter told them to do.

(Have one student read the verse, follow with discussion, and then have students paraphrase the verse on Scripture Sheet 5.)

Repentance comes before baptism. Repentance is being sorry, not only for the consequences of sin, but because you have gone against God. It's sorrow because you've hurt the relationship between you and God. Repentance also includes an action component of moving toward God and away from anything that messes up your relationship with Him. That's where your 100 percent commitment comes in again. The symbol of baptism represents repentance, which opens the floodgates of forgiveness.

Symbols can have more than one meaning. During World War II Winston Churchill, the prime minister of England, developed a symbol that caught on. It was the letter V, formed by raising one's index finger and middle finger. It symbolized an optimistic attitude of *victory*. Despite overwhelming attacks by the Germans, Churchill kept flashing the V sign, and it buoyed the hopes of the Allied Forces. Two decades later, Americans demonstrating for peace during the Vietnam War used the same symbol of the raised index finger and middle finger. But this time the symbol meant *peace*.

We find an additional meaning for the symbol of baptism in Acts 2:38. Baptism also represents the coming of the gift of the Holy Spirit into a believer's life. Since Jesus had returned to heaven, the gift of the Holy Spirit was a promise to His followers. Following Jesus by being baptized now also included receiving the gift of the Holy Spirit. So when you are baptized, it's not only for the forgiveness of sins but also to receive the gift of the Holy Spirit in your life.

III. JOHN 13:10, 14, 15: JESUS GAVE US THE SYMBOL OF SERVICE BY WASHING FEET.

Jesus initiated several religious symbols while He was on earth. One that Seventh-day Adventists follow is the washing of people's feet as part of the Communion service. The original story can be found in John 13:10, 14, 15.

(Have a student read the text, and then discuss it as a group. After this, have the students record their paraphrases of the passage on their Scripture Sheet 5. Then have them answer question 3 on their Work Sheet 5.)

Because people walked on dirt roads in those days, their feet became dusty and were washed by servants when they entered a house. At the time Jesus and the disciples met in the upper room, however, there were no servants. This made things awkward, since nobody wanted to be lowest on the totem pole by doing the work of a servant. So Jesus, the leader of the group, took the servant's position and washed the feet of the disciples. But He made it more than just washing dust off feet. He made it a symbol for His followers to serve others instead of trying to put themselves first.

Notice that people who have already washed don't need a complete bath; they need to have only their feet washed. In symbolic terms, this could be paraphrased, "Those who have been baptized by immersion to symbolize that all their sins have been washed away/forgiven don't need to be completely immersed when they sin again." Instead, they only need to have those sins forgiven, since their previous sins— committed prior to baptism—already were forgiven. In a sense, washing the feet is like a rebaptism. Those who think they will never sin again once they have been baptized must not know about the symbol of washing one another's feet. This act acknowledges that we still make mistakes and need forgiveness after we've been baptized.

Perhaps you've experienced a foot-washing service.

(Show students a typical foot-washing basin and the towels used to dry the feet.)

Sometimes it's awkward, not because we function as servants, but because we don't walk on dirt roads these days. So foot washing is not a common activity. Some people are embarrassed not only to wash somebody else's feet but also to have their own feet washed! Today we are servants both to wash somebody else's feet and to have our own washed. But the act can be very meaningful when you contemplate what the symbol means, which is much more than just the surface act of washing feet.

IV. 1 CORINTHIANS 11:23, 24: IN THE LORD'S SUPPER, BREAD SYMBOLIZES THE BODY OF CHRIST.

Ever since the death of Christ, Christians have remembered this solemn event through a symbolic service known as the Lord's Supper, sometimes called the Last Supper. It was the last meal Jesus ate with His disciples before His crucifixion. At this supper they were participating in the Jewish symbolic meal called the Passover, which reminded them of when the angel of death "passed over" all those in Egypt who had lamb's blood on their doorposts, another symbol that showed they trusted that the death of the innocent lamb would take their place. Jesus was the innocent one who died in our place, so the symbols now represent that He died for us.

Although the story can be found in several places in the Bible—Matthew 26:26-29; Mark 14:22-25; and Luke 22:19, 20—the well-known reference we're going to look up is in 1 Corinthians 11:23, 24. This is the way the Christians in the church at Corinth remembered the Lord's Supper.

(Have one student read the text, then ask how many have heard that passage read before. Ask what it means to them and ask them to explain the symbolism. Then have students write their own paraphrases on their Scripture Sheet 5.)

Jesus took the basic symbol of food—bread—and made it the symbol of His death. In other words, Jesus provides our basic needs. Jesus is the answer to the part of the Lord's Prayer that says "Give us this day our daily bread" (Matthew 6:11). Those who eat this symbol to fill up on calories will be greatly disappointed.

(Hold up a piece of Communion bread to demonstrate.)

It's smaller than a Wheat Thin and not as tasty. In fact, there's hardly any taste to it. Sometimes people serve larger portions at Communion services for youth. But remember, the purpose is not caloric intake; it's to remind us of the death of Jesus. The text doesn't say to do this whenever we feel like it, but to do it so we will remember what Jesus did for us. Seventh-day Adventists usually schedule a Communion service, the Lord's Supper, four times a year.

V. 1 CORINTHIANS 11:25, 26: IN THE LORD'S SUPPER, THE GRAPE JUICE SYMBOLIZES THE BLOOD OF CHRIST AND ANTICIPATES HIS RETURN ("UNTIL HE COMES").

Continuing our reading of the Lord's Supper, we discover another symbol Jesus instituted. It's found in the next two verses—1 Corinthians 11:25, 26.

(Have one student read the text, then discuss it as a group. Follow this up by having students write their paraphrases on their Scripture Sheet 5.)

The "new covenant" means God is living within our hearts and giving us the desire to follow Him. By contrast, the "old covenant" meant people could see and hear what God wanted, but did not have it inside where our motivations really start (see Jeremiah 31:31-34).

To have grape juice symbolize blood sounds a little gory. But that's because we tend to associate blood drinking with vampires. When Jesus instituted this symbol, the people of that time already associated blood with life (see Leviticus 17:11). In other words, to say the grape juice represents the blood of Jesus means the juice symbolizes Christ's life. How appropriate that we remember that He gave His life by taking that juice and making it part of our life! We do want Jesus on the inside of us!

But there's another symbolic meaning, too. When we participate in the Lord's Supper we not only remember that He died for us; we continue this service of remembering until Jesus returns. Within this symbol is the seed of hope that antici- pates the return of Christ (see Matthew 26:29).

(Have students respond to question 4 on their Work Sheet 5.)

Once again, we drink the juice, not to quench our literal thirst *(hold up a small Communion glass),* but as a symbol of making Christ's life a part of our own.

CONCLUSION:

Today we focused on symbols—things that represent much more than what they are literally. The major religious symbols are baptism, foot washing, and the Lord's Supper.

You circled choices for what baptism means. On your Work Sheet, I'd like you to write what baptism means to you, using your own words. I'm not looking for a tech- nically correct answer, but what it means to you.

(Give students time to create their own written responses. The concluding sec- tion of this study is an invitation for baptism. You may prefer to handle this on a one- to-one basis. When an adult and a young person enter into this type of dialogue, it's a delicate situation. Adults can easily intimidate young people. Sometimes our ea- gerness to see people make a commitment to Christ actually forces them to make a premature decision. When this happens, there can easily be hurt and anger later when the young person feels that a religious adult took advantage of him/her. Please use prayerful caution as you give this momentous invitation.)

At the bottom of your Work Sheet is a question that asks whether or not you want to be baptized and why. I want to make it clear that this is an invitation for you to be baptized. I'm doing this because I want you to have the opportunity to experience the symbol of having all your sins forgiven. I know you could go through the motions without really meaning it. I'm certainly not wanting to pressure you to do this. If you're not interested in giving yourself completely to God, don't do it. Maybe it's a decision you would prefer to make later. But if you are interested in making this major com- mitment at this time, I want you to know you have an invitation to say yes!

Take your time in responding to this last question, and please share your re- sponse with me. I'm interested in whatever you decide to do.

(Give the students time to respond thoughtfully; then close with prayer.)

SCRIPTURE SHEET 5
Symbols

1. Mark 1:4:

What it means: _____

_____

2. Acts 2:38:

What it means: _____

_____

3. John 13:10, 14, 15:

What it means: _____

_____

4. 1 Corinthians 11:23, 24:

What it means: _____

_____

5. 1 Corinthians 11:25, 26:

What it means: _____

_____

WORK SHEET 5
Symbols

1. **What do the following symbols mean?**

_____

_____

_____

_____

_____

(In the three multiple-choice questions below, circle the correct choices. There may be more than one correct answer.)

2. **What does baptism mean?**

   a. You need a bath.

   b. You want to start a new life with Jesus.

   c. You now want to choose to completely follow Jesus on your own.

   d. You will never do anything wrong again for the rest of your life.

3. **What does foot washing mean?**

   a. Your feet are dirty.

   b. You want to serve others.

   c. Nothing.

   d. You want forgiveness for recent sins.

4. What does the Communion service mean?

a. You want Jesus to come into your life again.

b. You want some food to eat before you get home.

c. You are looking forward to heaven.

d. You want to be better than everyone else.

5. What baptism means to me: _____

_____

_____

_____

_____

6. I want to be baptized: ○ Yes ○ No

Because: _____

_____

_____

FAMILY TALK BACK SHEET 5
Symbols

1. What are some of the reasons you've heard people give regarding why they were baptized? What do you think are good reasons to be baptized?

2. Have you ever asked for forgiveness? How can you tell if you're forgiven? How can others tell when you've forgiven them?

3. Do you have the Holy Spirit living in you? How do you know?

4. Some people call the foot-washing service the "ordinance of humility." What does that mean? Since we don't have servants who wash our feet these days, what would be another way to serve others with humility?

5. Why is the Communion service so serious? Why don't they have more food, especially since it is called the Lord's Supper?

6. If you were to make a symbol to remember that Jesus died for you, what symbol would you use for a reminder?

7. Why do you think Jesus gave us symbols such as baptism, foot washing, and the Lord's Supper?

Baptismal Study Guide Outline 6

SPIRITUALITY

Introduction: How to communicate with God.

I. Scriptures are from God and are for our good (2 Timothy 3:15-17).
    A. We can learn a lot from books. The Bible contains 66 books.
    B. The Bible teaches us about salvation.
    C. How the Bible was written.

II. First milk, then solid food, 1 Peter 2:2 (Hebrews 5:12-14).
    A. How many Bible stories do you know?
    B. It's time to go beyond information to understanding.
    C. Reading the Bible for yourself.
    D. Versions/translations of the Bible.

III. Communicate with God; the Lord's Prayer (Matthew 6:7, 9-15).
    A. What happens when we pray?
    B. The Lord's Prayer.
    C. Talking with God.

IV. Communication with God needs to be regular. Vine and branches (John 15:1, 4, 5).
    A. Taking personal responsibility for your spirituality.
    B. Your personal devotional life.
    C. Illustration of a plant and a branch.

V. Be ready to share Jesus with respect (1 Peter 3:15).
    A. Giving away what you have.
    B. Paraphrase of 1 Peter 3:15.
    C. Describing a friend; describing Jesus as a friend.

VI. Conclusion: Transition to spiritual responsibility by initiating contact with spiritual leaders and asking them to become spiritual supporters.

Baptismal Bible Study Guide 6

SPIRITUALITY

SCRIPTURE TEXTS:

1. 2 Timothy 3:15-17: God communicates with us through the Bible.
2. Hebrews 5:12-14: As we learn, we mature (1 Peter 2:2).
3. Matthew 6:7, 9-15: Prayer is part of our communication with God.
4. John 15:1, 4, 5: Make your spiritual development a regular part of your life.
5. 1 Peter 3:15: Be ready to share Jesus with others.

DECISION TIME:

Take personal responsibility for one's spiritual life.

MAKE IT CONCRETE (stage 3 appropriate):

Several books, including textbooks and reference books.

Jars of baby food to illustrate what's appropriate and what's not.

Copies of Bible translations and paraphrases.

A plant with branches that will die when they are cut off from the plant.

Collecting more than you can hold leads to dropping things and not being able to accept more—unless you give some away.

Have students tell you some of the neat things about their personal friend(s).

MATERIALS NEEDED:

Basic study tools for each student—Bible, workbook Scripture Sheet 6, workbook Work Sheet 6, pen or pencil.

School textbook.

Several bottles of baby food.

Several Bible translations and/or paraphrases.

A plant with small branches that can be broken off.

A bag of assorted items (more than one person can hold).

INTRODUCTION:

Have you ever wished you could talk to God face-to-face, the way Adam and Eve did before sin entered the world? I sure have! It makes me eager for Jesus to return so we can talk back and forth. I know God is eager for that too. In the meantime, though, how can we communicate with God? Since God made us, there is something deep inside us that doesn't feel right until we're in touch with Him. Some people call it their soul; others refer to it as their spirit. It's the inner part of who we are, who we are at the core. It's the part that most people don't know about us. And that part of us longs to be in contact with God.

74

I. 2 TIMOTHY 3:15-17: GOD COMMUNICATES WITH US THROUGH THE BIBLE.

A good teacher can teach us a lot. But some people learn from books. Through a book you can discover quickly what others have learned over a long period of time. It's like taking a shortcut to learning. Your parents have plenty to teach you when you are a child. But as you get older, you've learned a lot of what your parents have been teaching you and you're ready to go on to something more. That's where other teachers and books come in. Reading a book is a little like having your own teacher, except you can't ask questions or have a conversation with a book!

(Hold up one of the student's textbooks, and possibly one of your own books, to illustrate books as a source of information. Reference books are useful examples in this regard.)

One way God communicates with us is through books. In fact, He provided 66 books for our instruction. Some of these books are very short—less than one page. Others are much longer—more than 100 pages. All of them have been combined into one large book we call the Bible. Let's turn to 2 Timothy 3:15-17 and read where these books came from and what their purpose is.

(Have one student read the passage, then discuss the various purposes identified. Following the discussion, have students write their personal paraphrases of the passage on their Scripture Sheet 6.)

The Bible gives us the information we need for salvation. That's why we're using it as our textbook for this baptismal preparation class. Like Timothy, many of you have grown up with the Bible being used in your home. Your parents have taught you about God from information they received from Scripture. And not only does the Bible show us the way to salvation, it also trains us to be useful for good.

God didn't sit down and write the Bible one day. So how did the Bible get written?

(Field responses from students. Some may refer to 2 Peter 1:21 [holy men of God wrote as they were directed by the Holy Spirit]. Direct them to the first question on Work Sheet 6. Have them jot down notes during this discussion. Or you may opt for either an introductory or summary statement for this section.)

Actually, the 39 books in the Old Testament cover the history of God's people from the creation of the world to the first coming of Christ, the promised Messiah God's people were looking for as the way to salvation.

The earliest writers lived about 1,500 years before Christ was born. For more than 1,000 years different writers recorded messages God gave them. Some of these messages had information primarily for one particular time period. Messages that would carry God's instruction for more than one time period became part of the Bible. That's why it's important to have an understanding of the setting in which the message was first used. That can deepen its meaning as we apply it to our lives today. And the Bible continues to make sense for our situation, not just the world as it was thousands of years ago.

The 27 books in the New Testament give the story of the time Jesus was on earth and then tell the story of the development of Christianity after Jesus returned to heaven. Many of the books in the New Testament are actually letters the apostle Paul wrote to different churches or individuals, such as Paul's second letter to Timothy.

II. HEBREWS 5:12-14: AS WE LEARN, WE MATURE.

As we grow up we move from having our parents and other adults teach us everything about God to the point of understanding God for ourselves. Some young people think they've learned all there is to know once they become familiar with a bunch of Bible stories. They get a bored look on their faces when they begin to hear about David and Goliath, or even David and Bathsheba. They're not ready to begin to understand something deeper than the details of the story itself.

How about you? Are you already familiar with a lot of Bible stories? Do you do well when you play Bible trivia games? If so, you have a good foundation to go deeper. Are you ready to discover God for yourself instead of just through hearing the stories of others? Or do you want to still be a child when it comes to your spiritual life?

Hebrews 5:12-14 *(contrast with 2 Peter 2:2)* identifies this problem of people who fail to grow up in their spiritual lives.

(Have one student read Hebrews 5:12-14, then have another give a paraphrase of it. This passage is a little difficult for many to understand, so it might take a little time. When students are ready, have them write their own paraphrase of the passage on their Scripture Sheet 6.)

You probably can't remember the days before you had teeth. Most likely you were fed baby food.

(Pull out some jars of baby food to illustrate. Have a variety, and be prepared to feed some of the students.)

Some people secretly eat baby food even when they're older. Maybe even some of you do! Would anyone like some carrots? How about some peaches? Well, I'm sure all of us eat baby food when it comes to something like applesauce.

One of the keys to becoming mature in our spiritual lives is to be able to read and understand the Bible for ourselves. Most people your age are quite capable of actually reading the Bible, especially if it's a version that uses current English. But most are not able to understand it for themselves unless somebody else explains it to them. That's why we keep doing a paraphrase of each passage we study. I want you to be able not only to read the Bible, but to understand it for yourself. Sometimes it's hard work, but it's part of the process of maturity.

Do you have your own Bible?

(If you conduct these studies in a school setting, you may find that some students have one Bible at home and another one at school.)

Do you know what translation it is?

(Have students share which Bible version they have.)

Here's a critical question: Do you understand your version of the Bible when you read it?

(Have participants respond.)

On your Work Sheet, item 2, write down which Bible translation you like best.

(Give students time to write this on their Work Sheet. Some might not have their own Bible at this time. This gives you an opportunity to discuss a meaningful Bible version for them.)

I would encourage you to have a Bible you can understand; otherwise, it's not of much use to you except as a decoration or good-luck charm!

Some people get very agitated about which version of the Bible other people use. There are *translations* and there are *paraphrases.* A translation is a version of the Bible in which a number of people study the oldest copies of the Bible in the languages in which they were written—Hebrew, Greek, and a little bit of Aramaic. Then these scholars translate them into another language, such as English. The translators sometimes come from various denominations so that there won't be a bias toward one particular denomination. Examples of English translations are the New International Version (NIV), the Revised Standard Version (RSV), the King James Version (KJV), and the *New American Standard Bible* (NASB).

A popular way to understand the Bible is through the use of a paraphrase. Typically, a paraphrase is one person's restatement of the Bible in his or her own words. This person may or may not understand Hebrew, Greek, or Aramaic. Each of you have been doing a paraphrase of the various verses from the Bible in our study each week. Some examples of paraphrases are the *Living Bible* (TLB), *The Clear Word,* and *The Message.*

Let me make it clear that nobody has ever found the original Bible. The oldest copies we have are copies of copies of copies of copies. In recent years some older copies have been found, which results in some of the newer Bible translations being slightly more accurate than the older translations. But the differences usually are minimal. Seventh-day Adventists believe the ideas, not the specific words, are what are inspired. So if a few words are different but the basic idea is the same, what's the big deal? The most important thing is to *understand* the Bible you read.

III. MATTHEW 6:7, 9-15: PRAYER IS PART OF OUR COMMUNICATION WITH GOD.

Prayer is another way our spiritual lives develop. Most of us think of prayer as the thing we do before meals, possibly when we go to bed, and certainly when we get into an emergency situation. Very few of us think we're very good at praying. When we hear public prayers, such as those at church, they're usually different from the way we talk, so we figure we don't know how to pray. Some think there is a magical formula we must learn, or perhaps if we pray long enough we will get God's attention, as if God isn't really interested in us unless we start to bother Him. What happens when we pray? Take a few moments to jot down some of your ideas by item 3 on your Work Sheet.

(Give students time to write some of their ideas, and then lead a discussion about them.)

When Jesus was on earth, His followers asked Him to teach them to pray (Luke 11:1-4). His response is now called the Lord's Prayer. You probably have it memorized and can say it without even thinking about it. Even so, let's read it in Matthew 6:7, 9-15.

(Have a student read the passage, and encourage others to give their own paraphrase. You may prefer to have students write their own prayer on a blank sheet of paper. You also have the Scripture Sheets on which the students can write their own paraphrase of this passage.)

One thing certain about the Lord's Prayer is that Jesus instructed us to ask Him for the things we need. We also ask Him for the things we want. But as you mature, the asking moves beyond treating God like a Santa Claus or a magic genie. Our view of God blends the power of our Creator with the wisdom and gentleness of a lovable daddy and the closeness of a best friend. We then have regular conversations with God.

They may be short, perhaps a sentence or two. At other times they will be longer—maybe a couple minutes. You might even find yourself spending a long time thinking things through, being open to input from God. That's a type of prayer, too. Some carry on a silent conversation with God as they read their Bible—that's praying! Prayer isn't limited to formal words you say when kneeling, with hands folded and eyes closed—although that's a type of prayer, also.

The most important thing about prayer is not the words you use, when you do it, how long you pray, or what posture you have. The most important thing is simply to do it. The purpose is communication with God. Just try it and learn as you go. Take the plunge as you mature!

IV. JOHN 15:1, 4, 5: MAKE YOUR SPIRITUAL DEVELOPMENT A REGULAR PART OF YOUR LIFE.

When you are young, adults schedule your time for contact with God. They schedule and plan family worships, take you to Sabbath school and church, and possibly send you to a Christian school. But you've come to the point of taking responsibility for your own spiritual development. This doesn't mean you will no longer participate in family worship. Actually, you should probably ask to lead out once in a while. This doesn't mean you'll quit going to Sabbath school or church. The difference is that now you are the one primarily responsible for your own spirituality. You are choosing what others used to choose for you.

Jesus has a clue for you when it comes to being in charge of your spiritual life. It's the very counsel He gave to His disciples, and it can be found in John 15:4, 5.

(Have one student read the passage; have another one offer a paraphrase of it. Then have all the students record their paraphrases on their Scripture Sheet 6.)

Some people rely on the spiritual high from camp meeting, summer camp, a Pathfinder Camporee, or a mission trip to give them their spiritual input for a year or two. But it doesn't last that long. While there are ups and downs in our spiritual journeys, Jesus instructed us to stay in regular contact with Him. How can you be friends with somebody when you're never in contact with that person? That's just an imaginary friendship. Part of spiritual maturity is making time for your Friend, Jesus, even when you don't "feel" like it. In addition to spiritual highs from special events, to grow in your spirituality you need regular times for just you and Jesus. It's a way to keep centered on how to live for Jesus the rest of the time, too.

What happens if you don't have regular times with God? Your spiritual life dies. Just as you can't survive physically on one meal a week, so your spiritual life will starve unless it's fed. Another way to understand this is by observing what happens to part of a plant when it gets separated from the source of its nourishment.

(Bring out the plant and demonstrate by cutting off one of the branches.)

What will happen to this branch now that it's cut off from its source of nourishment?

(Have students respond. It would be worthwhile to leave the branch where the students can see it in a day or two and be reminded of this illustration.)

Some people make no time to spend with Jesus, and then they wonder why their spiritual life is so dead. Are they expecting others to be responsible for their spirituality instead of being responsible themselves?

V. PETER 3:15: BE READY TO SHARE JESUS WITH OTHERS.

Those who have a rich experience with Jesus find that unless they share what they have, their spiritual life goes stale. When you share what you have, you have room for more. Let me illustrate this by giving one of you a few things to hold.

(Select one student and hand that person one item at a time from your bag. Keep adding things until the person can't hold any more and begins to drop things. Then suggest he or she give some of the items to someone else. You can then give him/her more.)

So how do you "give away" your spiritual experience? By helping others and by telling people about what's going on (and what's not going on) in your spiritual life. You'll notice counsel in 1 Peter 3:15 tells us this very thing.

(Have one student read the verse, and then have someone else paraphrase it. There are three parts to the verse: The middle sentence is the focus, but the other sentences relate to it too. After discussing it, have all students write their own paraphrase of the verse on their Scripture Sheet 6.)

Think about one of your friends; then I want you to tell me about this friend. Tell me what you like about this person, what makes him or her interesting, and what you think I'd like about him or her. Who wants to go first?

(Have each student take a turn.)

Now take some time to think about your friendship with Jesus. What do you like about Him? What makes Him interesting? What do you think I'd like about Him? Tell me about Jesus as your friend.

(Have students take turns with this exercise, also. It's likely to be more difficult because they might not have experienced Jesus as a friend and because Jesus isn't as tangible as another human being.)

And don't forget the last part of the verse—to share Jesus with gentleness and respect. Forcing Jesus on others is a real turnoff, and it's hardly the way Jesus presented Himself to people! The last item on our Work Sheet gives us space to brainstorm some of the ways we can let others know about Jesus. Take some time to write down a few ideas, then we'll share them as a group.

(Give students time to work individually before you begin the group discussion. It would be helpful for you to have some examples of how you and others have shared Jesus. Be especially mindful of getting examples of people the same age as your students.)

CONCLUSION:

Our topic today has been spirituality. You're old enough to take responsibility for your own spiritual life. We've identified and discussed some of the ways your spirituality can develop. In one sense, when you choose to be baptized it symbolizes that you are now in charge of this part of your life, too. Others will still influence you, but you're in charge now. It's up to you to maintain your contact with God so that your spirituality will flourish. You're not alone in this; you're simply in charge of it for your life.

If you'd like to be the person primarily responsible for your spiritual life, I'd like for you to let those who have been primarily responsible know. This isn't to put them down, but to thank them for what they've done and to invite them to be a spiritual supporter now that you're in charge of your own spiritual life. This would include people such as parents, teachers, pastors, and other significant people who have been leading you spiritually. They'll become your supporters. I'll ask you next time how your conversation went with these people. If you'd like some help in getting started on this, I'm available for you to bounce off some ideas or to practice such a conversation. It's time for you to take responsibility for your spiritual life. You're mature enough to do it now!

(Close with prayer.)

SCRIPTURE SHEET 6
Spirituality

1. 2 Timothy 3:15-17:

What it means: _____

_____

2. Hebrews 5:12-14:

What it means: _____

_____

3. Matthew 6:7, 9-15:

What it means: _____

_____

4. John 15:1, 4, 5:

What it means: _____

_____

5. 1 Peter 3:15:

What it means: _____

_____

WORK SHEET 6
Spirituality

1. How did we get the Bible?

   _____

   _____

2. The Bible translation I like best right now is the _____

   _____

3. Some of the things that happen when we pray include:

   _____

   _____

   _____

4. Some of the ways we can let others know about Jesus are:

   _____

   _____

   _____

FAMILY TALK BACK SHEET 6
Spirituality

1. Which parts of the Bible do you like? Which parts don't you like? Why? How do you find the parts of the Bible you like?

2. Do you have a Bible of your own? How much time each week do you spend on your own reading of the Bible? How much do you rely on others to provide your spiritual input?

3. When will you be the person in charge of your own spiritual life? What role will parents, teachers, Sabbath school leaders and teachers, friends, and others play in your spiritual life?

4. What's an example of one of your typical prayers? Are you satisfied with your prayers? Explain.

5. Give examples of prayers that were answered and prayers that weren't answered (as far as you were concerned).

6. How real is God to you? How do you share this with others?

7. Is it easier to witness to friends and family members, or is it easier to witness to strangers? Why?

Baptismal Bible Study Guide Outline 7

SPIRITUAL GIFTS

Introduction: Follow up on conversation with spiritual supporters.

I. The gift of the Holy Spirit is given to the followers of Jesus (Acts 2:38).
   A. Followers of Jesus are not alone.
   B. God lives inside His people through the Holy Spirit.
   C. Where have you seen God the Holy Spirit in others?

II. The fruit of the Holy Spirit (Galatians 5:22, 23).
   A. How to know whether or not the Holy Spirit lives in you.
   B. Fruit takes time to develop.
   C. Illustration of the branch from the plant (Study 6).

III. The Holy Spirit gives spiritual gifts to each believer, as He determines (1 Corinthians 12:1, 7, 11).
   A. Gift for each participant.
   B. The Holy Spirit gives gifts to God's people.
   C. If you're a follower of Jesus, the Holy Spirit has "gifted" you.
   D. The Holy Spirit decides which gifts to give you.

IV. The purpose of spiritual gifts (Ephesians 4:12, 13).
   A. The purpose is to build up the body of Christ.
   B. Illustration of the puzzle pieces.
   C. Identifying your spiritual gifts.

V. God's people can expect the spiritual gift of prophecy (Joel 2:28).
   A. Send a messenger.
   B. Aaron was a prophet/messenger for Moses.
   C. God gives us messages through prophets.
   D. God's people can expect Him to communicate to them through the spiritual gift of prophecy.

VI. Conclusion: Ask God to develop spiritual fruit in your life; identify areas of spiritual giftedness.

Baptismal Bible Study Guide 7

SPIRITUAL GIFTS

SCRIPTURE TEXTS:
1. Acts 2:38: The gift of the Holy Spirit is given to the followers of Jesus.
2. Galatians 5:22, 23: The fruit of the Holy Spirit.
3. 1 Corinthians 12:1, 7, 11: The Holy Spirit gives spiritual gifts to each believer as He determines.
4. Ephesians 4:12, 13: The purpose of spiritual gifts is to build up the body of Christ.
5. Joel 2:28: God's people can expect the spiritual gift of prophecy.

DECISION TIME:
Ask the Holy Spirit to continue developing the "fruit of the Spirit" in the students' lives.

Begin to experiment to identify the gifts of the Spirit to build up the body of Christ.

MAKE IT CONCRETE (stage 3 appropriate):
A plant in bloom, illustrating the fruit of the Spirit.

A collection of wrapped gifts—one for each student.

Putting puzzle pieces together to make a complete picture.

Sending someone (a "prophet") with a message from you.

MATERIALS NEEDED:
Basic study tools for each student—Bible, workbook Scripture Sheet 7, workbook Work Sheet 7, pen or pencil.

A plant in bloom, preferably the one used from the previous study.

A collection of wrapped gifts—one for each student. These can be inexpensive items, preferably a variety of items to illustrate the diversity of spiritual gifts.

A puzzle (could be three-dimensional) with enough pieces to give each student one or more pieces. It would be fitting to have the puzzle form a church, a body, or a picture of Christ or the world.

INTRODUCTION:
Now that you're the person primarily responsible for your spiritual life, tell me about the conversations you had this week with the people in your life who were your spiritual supporters.

(Draw out the students to share their experiences. It's likely that some will need some encouragement to still follow through on this task. Others might be ready to take that step now, although they weren't during the previous study.)

I. ACTS 2:38: THE GIFT OF THE HOLY SPIRIT IS GIVEN TO THE FOLLOWERS OF JESUS.

You may have felt a little bit alone by taking the position of being in charge of your spiritual life. There's another powerful element you should be aware of. We read about it a few lessons ago. Let's look at that Bible verse again. Turn to Acts 2:38. Notice what happens to people who repent and are baptized.

(Have one student read the text, then have another one give a paraphrase of it. Focus on the gift of receiving the Holy Spirit. Then each student can record the para- phrase of this verse on Scripture Sheet 7.)

Now, that's amazing! God the Holy Spirit can live inside you. In fact, the Holy Spirit is already living inside you. And you thought the Holy Spirit was always invisi- ble! You can see evidence of the Holy Spirit's presence by noticing how other peo- ple live. Where have you seen the Holy Spirit?

(Have students respond. If possible, identify how you've seen the Holy Spirit in the lives of some of your students.)

This doesn't mean you have it all together. It means that the Holy Spirit shows Himself through you at times. And that's reason to celebrate!

II. GALATIANS 5:22, 23: THE FRUIT OF THE HOLY SPIRIT.

How can you know if the Holy Spirit lives in you? It's really quite simple. Galatians 5:22, 23 gives the answer. Look it up and write the answers on Work Sheet 7.

(Have students record their findings on their Work Sheets, then have them com- pare their lists. The diversity of translations can be helpful in this regard. Have stu- dents give some examples of these "fruits" of the Spirit. Then have them write their own paraphrases of these verses on their Scripture Sheet 7.)

Keep in mind that fruit takes a while to develop. You can't plant a seed and get fruit the next day! It takes time. Be on the lookout for the development of "spiritual fruit" in the lives of others. Tell them what you see. This isn't to give them a big head; it's to let them know that the Holy Spirit is working in their lives.

Remember our plant from our last Bible study?

(Bring out the plant from the previous Bible study.)

What happened to the branch that is no longer connected to the plant?

(Allow participants to respond.)

As you can see, some of the branches on this plant have produced their "fruit." For some plants, flowers are their "fruit." The flowers come naturally as long as the branches are connected to the plant. Living for Jesus isn't a matter of gritting our teeth and trying harder to be good. It's a matter of staying connected to Jesus and letting the Holy Spirit develop the "fruit of the Spirit" in our lives.

III. 1 CORINTHIANS 12:1, 7, 11: THE HOLY SPIRIT GIVES SPIRITUAL GIFTS TO EACH BELIEVER AS HE DETERMINES.

I've brought a little gift for each of you. It isn't much, but it symbolizes something.

(Give each student one of the wrapped gifts. Have them open the gifts.)

Some of you might be curious as to why I gave these to you. They're just something to encourage you on your spiritual journey. They symbolize the gifts the Holy Spirit gives you. When the Holy Spirit enters your life, not only does He begin to develop the fruit of the Spirit in your life, but He also gives you spiritual gifts. You'll find these mentioned in 1 Corinthians 12:1, 7, 11. Let's read these verses now.

(Have a different student read each verse. These are loaded with meaning. Discuss each verse with the students.)

The first verse shows that we can be informed about spiritual gifts—there is no need to be ignorant! Verse 7 indicates that every believer receives at least one gift. If you're a believer and have received the Holy Spirit, you're gifted! Verse 11 points out that the Spirit is the one who determines who receives which gifts. You don't determine what you receive. Remember, it's a gift!

The entire chapter of 1 Corinthians 12 deals with spiritual gifts. It's worth reading and studying. Chapter 14 continues the discussion. Placed right between chapters 12 and 13 is the "love chapter" of the Bible, 1 Corinthians 13. You can find a list of a variety of spiritual gifts in 1 Corinthians 12. Two other lists of the gifts of the Spirit can be found in Romans 12 and Ephesians 4. Go ahead and write these under item 2 on your Work Sheet so it's handy for future study. Some of the gifts of the Spirit include being an effective teacher, being someone with hospitality, having an unusually large amount of faith, having the ability to earn lots of money for God's cause, being helpful, being a good pastor, having an extraordinary ability to lead people to Jesus, having effectiveness in working with new cultures, and having good leadership ability. Have you seen people utilizing any of these gifts for God?

The three lists of spiritual gifts aren't identical. There are similarities and differences. For those who wonder why, it's because the Spirit gives whatever gifts are needed. Because the Holy Spirit is God, you can expect that whatever is needed will be provided by the Spirit. And isn't it exciting to think that the Spirit chooses to release this supernatural ability through you?

IV. EPHESIANS 4:12, 13: THE PURPOSE OF SPIRITUAL GIFTS IS TO BUILD UP THE BODY OF CHRIST.

Jesus returned to heaven after the Resurrection. He's still there. But He seems to keep popping up all over the world. How is that possible? It's through the Holy Spirit. He told His disciples this would happen (John 16:7; 14:12, 16). The fact that so many people follow Jesus when He is in heaven is evidence that the Holy Spirit is at work. And the ministry of Jesus continues on this earth through His followers. To carry this mission out, the Holy Spirit equips people with spiritual gifts.

Let's make sure the purpose of spiritual gifts is clear. Look up Ephesians 4:12, 13 in your Bibles.

(Have one student read these verses—verse 11 lists some of the gifts of the Spirit. Have students discuss what these verses mean. Let them compare various Bible translations for greater understanding. Then have them write a personal paraphrase on their Scripture Sheet 7.)

The basic purpose of the gifts of the Spirit is to build up the body of Christ. There are two ways to do this. One way is to bring people to the church—the body of Christ.

By adding people to the group, you are building up the body of Christ. The second way is to help those already in the church mature in their spiritual life. That also builds up the body of Christ. The task is enormous, but the resources are supernatural! And we get to be in the middle of the action—God working through us to build up His body!

I have several pieces to a puzzle that I'd like to distribute to you. It's not difficult, but I need you to work together to complete a picture using the puzzle pieces I give you.

(Hand out puzzle pieces to the students. Include each person and feel free to give each student more than one puzzle piece. Once the pieces have been distributed, ask the participants to work together to assemble the picture. Time them, if you want, to add some intensity to the experience. They're likely to be curious about what the picture is. You can create your own puzzle by taking a poster and cutting it into a number of pieces. The more pieces you have, the longer it will take to assemble the picture. A puzzle of 20 to 25 pieces is recommended. Note how the group works together. Do they function well as a body? Feel free to comment on this after they complete their task.)

Sometimes it seems easier to do a project by yourself rather than involving others. Some projects are more efficient that way. But when it comes to the body of Christ, the Holy Spirit has decided to spread out the gifts. Each person in the body of Christ is needed. You can see that the fruits of the Spirit are needed as we minister to others through the gifts of the Spirit!

You can know that the Holy Spirit develops all of the fruits of the Spirit in your life *(refer to the first item on the Work Sheet).* But the gifts of the Spirit are distributed throughout your church. What part do you play in the puzzle? What spiritual gifts do you have?

(Ask the students to identify which gifts they have. Most won't think they have any. Because of their youthfulness and potential lack of awareness of spiritual gifts, they might not have a clue which spiritual gifts they have.)

Would you like to know which spiritual gifts you've been given to build up the body of Christ? Here are a few simple steps that will help you to discover them. First of all, what are the likely types of spiritual gifts you'd be given? While the Spirit can give you a gift in an instant, frequently He develops this gift within you over time. Are you aware of some of these special abilities? Perhaps it's something in the area of music, drama, or speaking. Maybe it's social skills, working behind the scenes, or leadership. What special abilities are developing in your life? While talents are special abilities God gives you at birth and are developed during your life, spiritual gifts have a focus on building up the body of Christ and may be developed over time or given instantly. A person may have the talent of singing, but not use it to build up the body of Christ. A spiritual gift of singing is for building up the body of Christ. What are some likely areas in which the Spirit has given you spiritual gifts?

The second step to take as you identify your spiritual gifts is really lots of fun. It calls for you to begin experimenting. Start to experiment for competence in a likely area of giftedness. For example, if you think you might have the gift of singing, experiment by trying it. Where can you sing to build up the body of Christ? Go try it! If the Spirit has given you that gift, you'll be able to do it. That doesn't mean you can do it perfectly the first time. But if God has given you the gift, you can do it!

As you experiment, see if you experience joy. When God is ministering through you to others, you experience joy. You're one of the avenues for Jesus to reach others! If you try serving at a soup kitchen and find it's a complete drag, experiment in other areas. Maybe you're gifted in serving children, or possibly helping the elderly or those with disabilities. Perhaps you experience joy when performing in front of a group of people. Or do you find greater satisfaction working behind the scenes to make things happen without a hitch? Experiment for joy.

And while you're experimenting, note whether or not there is success. Don't use a worldly measurement of success. The standard we're using is whether or not the use of your spiritual gift builds up the body of Christ. When God acts, there is success. Are you building up the body of Christ?

The final step in identifying your spiritual gifts is getting feedback from members of the body of Christ. Do others within the body notice that God has gifted you in the areas in which you're experimenting? You can't identify your spiritual gifts for the body without getting input from within the body!

Are you ready for go for it? Let's start experimenting!

(Help your students begin to identify their spiritual gifts based on their reception of the Holy Spirit and following the five steps listed above: identify your gifts, experiment, experience joy, experience success, get feedback.)

V. JOEL 2:28: GOD'S PEOPLE CAN EXPECT THE SPIRITUAL GIFT OF PROPHECY.

(Send one of the students in your group with a message for someone in another room, such as informing a teacher that your group will complete their study for the day in 10 minutes. This student is functioning as a "prophet" for you by speaking on your behalf.)

One of the many spiritual gifts is the gift of prophecy. What do you think of when you hear about prophecy?

(Field responses from students. Some will think of predicting the future, which is only one type of prophecy. Many won't have any idea.)

Do you remember what happened when God revealed Himself to Moses at the burning bush in the desert? Moses didn't want to return to Egypt. His last excuse was that he couldn't speak the language anymore. God had anticipated that one. Aaron, Moses' brother, was already on his way to meet Moses. God told Moses that he should give his messages to Aaron, and Aaron would pass them on to Pharaoh. The word used to describe this process is that Aaron would be the spokesperson for Moses (see Exodus 4:16).

A prophet is merely a spokesperson for God. I sent one of our students to deliver a message for me. That person was a "prophet" for me. When a person is a prophet for God, that person has received a message from God and delivers it to others. Sometimes it's a message for one specific person. At other times it's a message for a group of people. The message might be spoken; it might be written. Our Bibles are a collection of messages God gave to prophets. Go ahead and write your description of a prophet on your Work Sheet.

Because sin separated us from face-to-face communication with God, He initiated contact with us by sending us messages through prophets. When Jesus was on earth He gave God's messages directly, since He was God (see Hebrews 1:1, 2). And now that Jesus is back in heaven, He continues to send messages through prophets. It's one of the gifts the Spirit gives so that God's messages continue to be delivered to His people.

Wouldn't you expect God to communicate with His people? Let's turn to Joel 2:28 and read it.

(Have one student read the passage, then have everyone write his or her own paraphrase on Scripture Sheet 7.)

Seventh-day Adventists have an incredible collection of messages from a prophet who provided valuable input during the formation of the Seventh-day Adventist Church. We take that as an affirmation that the spiritual gift of prophecy was given to us too.

But according to our text, we can expect lots of people to receive that gift. Their messages might not be for an entire denomination. They might be for the church you attend or for some individuals within that church. I hope that when the pastor gives a sermon, it's a message from God and that the preacher has the gift of being a prophet for God to those who listen. I can't help wondering which of you will be given the spiritual gift of being a prophet. The Spirit will decide. Are you open to receiving that gift and others as well?

CONCLUSION:

The followers of Jesus are given the Holy Spirit, who lives inside us. By staying connected to God, the Holy Spirit develops the "fruit" of the Spirit in your life. Let's take a moment for silent prayer so you can ask God to develop this fruit in your life.

(After an appropriate pause, continue.)

There's another action of the Holy Spirit, in addition to developing spiritual fruit in your life. The Holy Spirit also gives spiritual gifts so that His people can continue the work Jesus did while He was here and build up the body of Christ. Please tell me some of the areas you will begin to experiment in to identify your spiritual gifts.

(Help students identify probable areas of giftedness and then seek opportunities to experiment for competence, joy, success, and affirmation from the body.)

SCRIPTURE SHEET 7
Spiritual Gifts

1. Acts 2:38:

What it means: _____

_____

2. Galatians 5:22, 23:

What it means: _____

_____

3. 1 Corinthians 12:1, 7, 11:

What it means: _____

_____

4. Ephesians 4:12, 13:

What it means: _____

_____

5. Joel 2:28:

What it means: _____

_____

WORK SHEET 7
Spiritual Gifts

1. What are the *fruits* of the Spirit?

_____   _____

_____   _____

_____   _____

_____   _____

_____   _____

2. Where in the Bible are the three lists of the *gifts* of the Spirit?

_____   _____

_____

3. What is a prophet?

_____

_____

FAMILY TALK BACK SHEET 7
Spiritual Gifts

1. What does the Holy Spirit do in your life? in the church? in the rest of the world?

2. Which fruits of the Spirit (Galatians 5:22, 23) are the most developed in your life? Which ones are getting or needing special attention right now? How does the Holy Spirit develop these fruits in your life?

3. What is the reason the Holy Spirit provides us with spiritual gifts (Ephesians 4:12, 13)? Describe examples of spiritual gifts you've seen and how they were used.

4. What spiritual gifts does it seem the Holy Spirit has given you? How have you used them? What has been the results?

5. What spiritual gifts have you seen others use? What will you do to let them know you've seen those spiritual gifts in them?

6. Discuss the spiritual gift of prophecy. What messages have you received from prophets? How does God send us messages today? Why would God want His people to have the spiritual gift of prophecy?

7. Read all of 1 Corinthians 12 (there are 31 verses) from a version of the Bible you like and can understand well. What are three key elements that stand out for you in this chapter?

Baptismal Bible Study Outline Guide 8

THE STATE OF THE DEAD

Introduction: What do you remember about funerals?

I.   God gives life: dust + breath/spirit = living soul (Genesis 2:7).
    A. The Bible gives us the equation.
    B. Illustration of the box.
    C. God is the source of life.

II. The first lie: "You won't die!" (Genesis 3:4).
    A. Paraphrase of Genesis 3:4.
    B. Other forms of the lie: reincarnation, burn in hell forever, everyone goes to heaven.

III. Dust to ground, spirit to God, no more person (Ecclesiastes 12:7).
    A. The equation goes in reverse.
    B. The box illustration.
    C. Talking to "spirits" that have died.

IV. Jesus said that death is like sleep (John 11:11-14).
    A. The story of Lazarus.
    B. Dead alive, dead dead, alive dead, alive alive.
    C. Illustration of car battery.

V.   Resurrections at the second and third comings of Christ (1 Thessalonians 4:13, 16-18).
    A. How do you respond at funerals?
    B. What happens when Jesus returns the second and third times?
    C. Death or sleep?

VI. Conclusion: Accept eternal life from Jesus.

Baptismal Bible Study Guide 8

THE STATE OF THE DEAD

SCRIPTURE TEXTS:
1. Genesis 2:7: God gives life: dust + breath/spirit = living soul.
2. Genesis 3:4: The first lie: "You won't die!"
3. Ecclesiastes 12:7: Dust to ground; spirit to God; no more person.
4. John 11:11-14: Jesus said that death is like sleep. Believers never die.
5. 1 Thessalonians 4:13, 16-18: Resurrections at the second and third comings of Christ.

DECISION TIME:
Choose to be alive in Christ.
Release the fear of death.
Have hope in the return of Jesus.

MAKE IT CONCRETE (stage 3 appropriate):
Boards and nails to illustrate the formation of a soul.
Battery-powered car to illustrate death as sleep.

MATERIALS NEEDED:
Basic study tools for each student—Bible, workbook Scripture Sheet 8, workbook Work Sheet 4, pen or pencil.

Boards and nails (or screws), plus a hammer (or screwdriver) to construct and dismantle a small box.

A small battery-operated car (or plane or flashlight) with both dead batteries and charged batteries.

INTRODUCTION:
Have you ever been to a funeral?

(Allow students to respond. Be aware that this could be a sensitive subject to some and somewhat of a joke to others.)

What do you remember about it?

(Again, have students respond.)

And now the question that people have asked for thousands of years: What happens to people after they die?

(Solicit responses from students and find out if anything was said at funerals they've attended regarding what happens to people after they die.)

Death rarely is a pleasant topic. Most people fear death. When we hear that someone has died, the most common reaction is denial: "No, it can't be!" In fact, most of us don't think we will die. Surprise! *Unless Jesus returns first, you are going to die!* And it might be before you turn 70. Isn't that shocking?

I. GENESIS 2:7: GOD GIVES LIFE: DUST + BREATH/SPIRIT = LIVING SOUL.

Instead of guessing what happens to people after they die, let's start with how people began. That takes us back to the Creation story and the origin of Adam and Eve. Turn to Genesis 2:7 in your Bible.

(Have one student read the verse, then have everyone write a paraphrase on Scripture Sheet 8.)

We can make this verse into a simple mathematical equation. When God created the first person He took *dust* and added His *breath.* Another word for breath is spirit. The Hebrew word *neshamah* means breath or life. The Greek word *pneuma* means breath or spirit, and is used in the New Testament and in the Septuagint—the Greek translation of the Old Testament.

So we have *dust* plus *breath.* The result is that the human becomes a *living soul.* The final equation is: dust plus breath equals a living soul.

(Have students fill in the blanks for the first item on Work Sheet 8.)

We can illustrate this equation with these pieces of wood and nails (or screws).

(Demonstrate the construction of a small box by arranging small boards into the shape of a box and then pounding in nails [or placing screws] to keep it together. You will disassemble the box later in the study, so don't make it too permanent!)

The *dust,* represented by the boards, comes from the ground; the *breath,* represented by the nails or screws, comes from God, the source of life; and the *living soul,* represented by the box, is a result of the first two coming together.

There have always been people who have thought that we are spirits floating around and then jumping into bodies. But "spirit" is simply breath from God. God is the source of life, not some floating spirit. Was the box we made floating around before it became a box? Did it come from heaven? Did it come from hell? No, it didn't even exist until we put the boards and nails or screws together.

Adam and Eve didn't know each other in some previous life. They didn't exist until God Himself formed them out of dirt—He was quite a sculptor!—and breathed life into them.

Although your parents conceived you, we could also say that you are the unique combination of dirt and God's life-giving breath. The result is you—a living soul. Before you were conceived, your personality and thought processes weren't desiring a body for lodging, like some snail mass looking for a house. God put the two elements together, and the result is you!

God created humans by breathing His life-giving spirit into them, and He provided a tree of life in the Garden of Eden (Genesis 2:9). But He also placed the tree of the knowledge of good and evil in the garden with a warning not to eat from it; otherwise they would die (verse 17). Because God is the source of life, attempts to exist without God result in death. If God were not the source of life, we could live without Him—as if we would want to.

II. GENESIS 3:4: THE FIRST RECORDED LIE: "YOU WON'T DIE!"

But a number of people try to live without God. Perhaps they believe the very first lie recorded on this earth. We can read it in Genesis 3:4.

(Have a student read it.)

This might be a little simplistic, but would you believe what God says, or what a talking snake says? Maybe the Source of life is holding out on us! Maybe we *can* live apart from God. Maybe we won't die!

All we need to do is check the evidence. Has anyone died since Adam and Eve ate the fruit? Did eating the fruit make us more like God when we already had been formed in His image? I suppose now we know more—we know the pain that comes with sin, including death.

(Have students write their own paraphrases to the verse on their Scripture Sheets.)

But people keep believing the lie today. "You won't die. You'll come back as a cow or a fly or a dog. You might come back as another person and live life all over again." Some people believe that your reincarnation depends on how good you've been. If you've been bad, you'll come back as a rat or a pig; if you've been good, you'll come back as a human with better circumstances in life—richer, wiser, better looking, more talented, more friends, etc.).

Other people believe you have only one chance on this earth. If you're good, you go to heaven; it you're bad, you go to hell. Since they believe that everyone lives forever, it's just a matter of whether that "forever" will be in heaven or in hell. And then there are others who don't like any talk about hell—it's just too depressing. So they kind of figure that everyone goes to heaven after they die, and there we get to continue our earthly experience with everyone in heaven. We'll probably have wings and float around on clouds, play harps, and slide down the necks of giraffes. Every once in a while we'll sneak back to earth and get involved in people's lives. Then we'll be zapped back to heaven and watch from a distance. That's the vague idea many people have regarding what happens when we die.

III. DUST TO GROUND; SPIRIT TO GOD; NO MORE PERSON.

Just as the Bible tells us how we began, the Bible also explains what happens to us after we die. It's a little bit like putting a movie in rewind. We can read about it in Ecclesiastes 12:7.

(Have one student read the text, and allow the others to comment on it before they write their own paraphrases on their Scripture Sheets.)

That's pretty straightforward! The dust returns to the ground, and the spirit, or breath, returns to God, who gave it.

What happens to the soul?

(Have students respond.)

Did the soul go to heaven? Did it go to hell? Is it floating around? Will it come and visit you? If when you walked past the casket at a funeral or when you attended a "viewing" at a funeral home you looked at the dead person's face, it's obvious that the soul wasn't there. Should we just assume that the soul is "hanging out" someplace else? Where has it gone?

Let's consider the box we constructed earlier. Putting the boards, or the dust, and the nails, or breath of life, together resulted in a box, the living soul. To reverse this box-making process, we simply remove the nails from the boards.

(Go ahead and do this.)

The result is a stack of boards, or dust, and a collection of nails, or breath of life. Where did the box go? Is it in heaven? Is it in hell? Is it floating around someplace? Where did it go?

(Have students respond.)

It simply stopped existing.

Some people claim to have talked to people who have died and are now part of the spirit world. If someone close to you died and later appeared to you out of thin air, the impact on you would be phenomenal! You might be overjoyed to see the person again. But according to the Bible, that person won't exist again until the resurrection.

"But he was real; I talked to him," you may insist.

Don't ever doubt that this interaction actually happens to people. The scary thing is the "spirit" they see is probably just like the loved one they miss so much. But their loved one didn't come back from heaven or from floating around. For thousands of years the devil has worked through sorcery and witchcraft to imitate people. The best thing to do is to stay away from it (Deuteronomy 18:9-12) and command the devil not to mess with you if such a thing happens to you (James 4:7).

The fact that we simply cease to exist when we die could make us feel completely insignificant—little more than a computer blip—if it weren't for additional information the Bible gives us about death. Let's take a look at that now.

IV. JESUS SAID THAT DEATH IS LIKE SLEEP. BELIEVERS NEVER DIE.

Turn to John 11:11-14. This is the story of Lazarus.

(Have one student read the passage; ask the class what this means, and what they think of death. Then have them write their own paraphrases on their Scripture Sheets.)

I think I probably would have been at least as confused as the disciples. If a sick friend is getting some sleep, that could help him get well. What a shock to hear that sleep is the same as death!

If that's true, how would you explain what Jesus told Martha in John 11:25, 26?

(Have students read it and then have them respond.)

Right now, are you dead or alive?

(Allow students to respond.)

Perhaps we need to clarify which death or life we're talking about. Since the Bible speaks of two types of life and two types of death, it seems possible to be dead while you're alive or alive while you're dead. Does that make sense?

Sometimes we limit our view of life merely to the time we're on this planet. Jesus thinks in terms of all eternity. People can be dead—living without God (Ephesians 2:1)—while they are alive and their heart is beating. Or people can be alive—given eternal life (John 3:16; 1 John 5:12)—while they are dead, or "asleep," because their heart isn't beating. You could be dead dead or you could be alive alive. Which combination are you right now?

(Allow students to respond.)

When you give your life to Jesus, He gives you everlasting life. You might sleep, or die, before He returns, but you have everlasting life.

When Jesus spoke of death as sleep, He used a term we can easily understand. We've all slept. We know that events occur while we're asleep, but since we are still alive, we'll soon be awake and continue "living." We could also compare the sleeping kind of death to a car with a dead battery.

(Pull out a small battery-operated car that has a dead battery. A battery-powered plane or even a flashlight will serve the same purpose.)

Just because the battery is dead doesn't make the car useless. It's just a matter of installing a new battery or recharging the existing one.

(Insert a new or recharged battery.)

V. 1 THESSALONIANS 4:13, 16-18: RESURRECTIONS AT THE SECOND AND THIRD COMINGS OF CHRIST.

If we die, sleep, before Jesus returns, many people will be sad. If you've been to a funeral, you've seen all the sad people. You've probably been sad too. It's heartbreaking to be separated from someone we care about, especially if it's someone close to us. Even though we will see those people again at the end of this world and the beginning of the next, it's sad to be apart from them now, while they sleep. But can you imagine what it's like for people at a funeral who have no hope in the resurrection? It really is all over for them. Their separation is final instead of like sleep.

Paul wrote about death, resurrection, and the return of Jesus. Let's read about it in 1 Thessalonians 4:13, 16-18.

(Have one student read only verse 13 and comment on it.)

Paul uses the same term for death as Jesus did—sleep. There's no need to be ignorant about what happens when we die, and there's no need to grieve the same way as those who don't have any hope of the resurrection. Sure, there will be grief when a person dies, but it's not the same as the grief of those with no hope of the resurrection!

Notice the blanks we still have on our worksheets. We'll fill in some of that information now.

(Continue by having a student read verses 16-18. Then have all the students write their paraphrases on the Scripture Sheets.)

We read some of this text when we studied about the return of Jesus. One of the events that happen when Jesus returns is that those who have accepted the gift of eternal life will be resurrected and taken to heaven. We don't go to heaven when we die. We sleep. The heaven part doesn't happen until Jesus returns. He takes all of His followers back to heaven at that time—those who are living when He returns as well as those who are "sleeping" (see Revelation 20:4-6).

What about those who haven't accepted God's gift of eternal life? What happens to them? In our earlier study about the return of Jesus we discovered that those people die when Jesus returns (2 Thessalonians 1:8-10; 2:8). And we also discussed the 1,000-year period called the millennium. We discovered that 1,000 years after the second coming of Christ there will be a third coming in which Jesus, all His followers, and the New Jerusalem will come to earth. Satan will be set free from his prison of earth and will lead all those opposed to God in one more attempt to defeat Jesus. But fire will come down from heaven and destroy them all forever. The Bible refers to this destruction as the "second death" (Revelation 20:14).

You and I might experience the "first death," which is merely sleep. Others would feel sad to be separated from us until Jesus returns. But the bigger deal is the second death. That is the death that Jesus went through for us. Because we accept the gift of eternal life from Jesus, neither you nor I will have to experience that death.

CONCLUSION:

Would you like to confirm or reconfirm your decision to accept eternal life from Jesus so that you will never die?

(Allow students to respond.)

If you have eternal life, that frees you from being consumed about whether or not you will die. No wonder so many people have been willing to die for Jesus. They were certain they had eternal life, so what difference did a "moment" of sleep make to them? Because you have Jesus, you have eternal life. That fact removes the natural fear of death so many people have and frees us to really live for Jesus!

SCRIPTURE SHEET 8
The State of the Dead

1. Genesis 2:7:

What it means: _____

_____

2. Genesis 3:4:

What it means: _____

_____

3. Ecclesiastes 12:7:

What it means: _____

_____

4. John 11:11-14:

What it means: _____

_____

5. 1 Thessalonians 4:13, 16-18:

What it means: _____

_____

WORK SHEET 8
The State of the Dead

1. The equation for the creation of humans is:

   _____ + _____ = _____

2. When a person says he or she talked to someone who has died, to whom was he or she probably talking?

   _____

   _____

3. How many deaths are there?_____

4. When do these deaths happen?

   _____

   _____

5. How many resurrections are there? _____

6. When do these resurrections happen?

   _____

   _____

FAMILY TALK BACK SHEET 8
The State of the Dead

1. What happens to people when they die? How do you know? Why is there even such a thing as death?

2. Why are there so many different beliefs about what happens to people when they die—such as reincarnation, heaven, purgatory, sleep, hell, spirits or ghosts?

3. How old do you think you will be when you die? Would you feel cheated if you died before reaching this age? Do you know of persons who died before they thought they would? Who or what determines how old you will be when you die?

4. Why are so many people afraid to die? What percentage of the people you know will die?

5. Compare what humans think of when it comes to death (Ecclesiastes 9:5) with what God thinks of when it comes to death (John 11:11-14, 25, 26).

6. How do you respond to stories about people communicating with dead people? How do you respond to the near-death stories about traveling down a long tunnel that has a light at the end?

7. When does eternal life begin for Christians (John 5:24)? How does that make a difference regarding a person's death and resurrection? How does "giving your life to Jesus" relate to all this?

THE SANCTUARY AND THE THREE ANGELS' MESSAGES

Introduction: Create a thank-you card.

I.   The sanctuary on earth was similar to the one in heaven (Hebrews 8:1, 2, 5).
     A. The sanctuary on earth was built so God could dwell with His people.
     B. Symbols of the earthly sanctuary.
     C. What the symbols represent in heaven.

II. The heavenly sanctuary was "cleansed" after 2300 days/years (Daniel 8:14).
     A. New England on October 22, 1844.
     B. The prophecy of Daniel 8:14.
     C. Sanctuary = heaven; cleansed = restored/made right, judgment.

III. First angel's message: The gospel to everyone; respect God, give Him glory, and worship Him; the judgment of God has come (Revelation 14:6, 7).
     A. Components of the first angel's message.
     B. Paraphrase of Revelation 14:6, 7.
     C. Interruption of the "loud voice."

IV. Second angel's message: God's enemy will lose (Revelation 14:8).
     A. The symbols of this message.
     B. The meaning today.
     C. You can know who wins and who loses!

V.   Third angel's message: Bad news for God's enemies; God's people will need patience (Revelation 14:9-12).
     A. God's wrath.
     B. Need for patience by God's people.

VI. Conclusion: It will take serious commitment to get out the word about the three angels' messages. Thank God for what is symbolized by the sanctuary.

Baptismal Bible Study Guide 9

THE SANCTUARY AND THE THREE ANGELS' MESSAGES

SCRIPTURE TEXTS:
1. Hebrews 8:1, 2, 5: The sanctuary on earth was similar to the one in heaven.
2. Daniel 8:14: The heavenly sanctuary was "cleansed" after 2300 days/years.
3. Revelation 14:6, 7: First angel's message: the gospel to everyone; respect God, give Him glory, and worship Him; the judgment of God has come.
4. Revelation 14:8: Second angel's message: God's enemies will lose.
5. Revelation 14:9-12: Third angel's message: bad news for God's enemies; God's people will need patience.

DECISION TIME:
Be part of getting out the word from the three angels.
Prayer of gratitude for what Jesus does for us as symbolized in the sanctuary.

MAKE IT CONCRETE (stage 3 appropriate):
Different ways of saying thank you.
Pictorial diagram of the wilderness sanctuary.
Action photograph of someone you know but whom the group doesn't know.
Interruption of Bible study by a person who enters and loudly proclaims a message.
Magazine or newspaper predictions, such as who will win a sports championship, along with a report of what really happened.

MATERIALS NEEDED:
Basic study tools for each student—Bible, workbook Scripture Sheet 9, workbook Work Sheet 9, pen or pencil.
Colored paper and pens for creating homemade thank-you cards.
Action photograph of someone you know but whom the students don't know.
Make arrangements for someone to interrupt the Bible study loudly at a given signal.
Copy of a magazine or newspaper prediction, such as who will win a sports championship, along with a report of what actually happened.

INTRODUCTION:
In one of our earlier Bible studies we considered various symbols and what they mean. Which symbols do you remember?
(Have students recall which symbols they remember, as well as what they mean.)
Today we're going to create our own symbols and discover other symbols God

gave us to increase our understanding about Him and what He's about.

I'd like for you to think of somebody you'd like to thank.

(Give students time to think of somebody.)

You could walk up to them and say "Thank you." And we've all done that many times. But let's be a little more creative. What are some other ways you could communicate appreciation?

(Have students brainstorm additional ways of giving thanks. Be prepared to give some examples to get them going.)

One way to communicate your gratitude is to send a person a thank-you card. You can buy these by the box and send them out whenever you get the urge. But today we're going to do the old, homemade type of thank-you card. You probably did these when you were a kid. Maybe some of you still do it. Such a card is very personal when it's homemade. Go ahead and create a thank-you card for the person you want to thank. Make it one of your originals!

(Give students about six to nine minutes to create their thank-you cards. Encourage them to make them original—something uniquely from them.)

Notice the different ways of communicating a simple message. What do these various cards communicate, in addition to "Thank you"?

I. HEBREWS 8:1, 2, 5: THE SANCTUARY ON EARTH WAS SIMILAR TO THE ONE IN HEAVEN.

God used symbols to communicate with His people. When He instructed Moses to build a sanctuary so He could dwell with His people (Exodus 25:8), He said to make it like a tent, just as the people lived in tents. Later, when Solomon built a Temple for God, it was a permanent structure, just as the people now had permanent houses and were no longer wandering through the desert. But God also made sure that certain symbols were included in the sanctuary as another way to share more about Himself with His people.

Notice the description we find in Hebrews 8:1, 2, 5.

(Have one person read the verses and then open the discussion for verbal paraphrases. This can be a little complicated, since the context is the superiority of Jesus as the high priest of a new and better covenant. However, these verses point out that the superiority of the heavenly parts presupposes the existence of the earthly counterparts.)

You may have heard about how the priests in the Old Testament functioned as a connecting point between God and His people. The priests' work pointed forward to the coming of Jesus, who would be the one who connects us to God.

And God had some very specific directions for what His sanctuary would be like. The sanctuary on earth was to be similar to the one in heaven, a copy or pattern—from the Hebrew word *tabnith* (Exodus 25:9; 1 Chronicles 28:19) and the Greek word *tupos* (Hebrews 8:5). Look at this diagram of the desert sanctuary. As you copy it on your Work Sheets, notice what each item symbolizes.

(While you draw the diagram on the whiteboard or flipchart, students draw one on Work Sheet 9. Take time for discussion on these items. Part of the purpose of the

various parts of the sanctuary was to communicate certain aspects of God on a regular basis. That's one reason symbols are powerful. Don't fall into the literalism trap of the candlestick in heaven looking just like the candlestick of the wilderness tabernacle. Solomon's Temple had 10 of them: five on the south side and five on the north side [2 Chronicles 4:7]. Remember, Jesus was pictured by John as walking among the seven candlesticks [Revelation 1:12, 13].

These are the symbols of the desert sanctuary:
Altar of burnt offering = the death of Jesus.
Laver = forgiveness of sins and baptism.
Table of shewbread = Jesus as the bread of life.
Candlestick = Jesus as the light of the world.
Altar of incense = Jesus as our prayer intercessor.
Ark = the throne of God.
The courtyard = the atonement of Christ.
The first compartment of the sanctuary = the intercessory work of Christ.
The second compartment of the sanctuary = the judgment.
Have students write paraphrases on their Scripture Sheets.)

We haven't seen God face-to-face. But we can find out a lot about God, especially what He does for us, just by understanding the symbolic sanctuary He designed. It's something like you trying to find out about a friend of mine. You might not have seen my friend, but by looking at this photo of him, what can you discover about my friend?

(Show an action photo of a friend of yours and note what the students discover simply from one photo. Choose a photo that does communicate a lot.)

II. DANIEL 8:14: THE HEAVENLY SANCTUARY WAS "CLEANSED" AFTER 2300 DAYS/YEARS.

Just before the Seventh-day Adventist Church began, many people in the New England states were convinced that the second coming of Jesus would occur on October 22, 1844. Why did they have this conviction? How did they arrive at this date?

One significant verse that led them to this conclusion was Daniel 8:14. Let's read that verse.

(Have a student read the verse, then ask the students what they think it means.)

The keys words are "2300 days," "sanctuary," and "cleansed." When the Bible speaks in a symbolic way, as it does in a large part of the books of Daniel, Revelation, and Ezekiel, a day usually stands for a year (see Ezekiel 4:6 and Numbers 14:34). So the 2300 days symbolize 2300 years. By calculation with the predictive prophecies in Daniel 9, the 2300 years concluded on October 22, 1844.

The sanctuary written about in Daniel 8:14 is the sanctuary in heaven. Those expecting the return of Jesus in 1844 made the mistake of thinking the sanctuary Daniel was talking about was the earth. They thought Jesus was returning to earth at that time to cleanse it.

The word translated "cleansed" is rarely used in the Bible, which makes it difficult to make comparisons of how it is used. It could be translated in several ways: just, right, cleansed, pure, or restored. Additional study has led Seventh-day Adventists to understand this to mean a judgment before the second coming of Jesus. Satan has accused God of not being fair and has accused us of not being worthy of heaven. God sets everything out so that even created beings from others worlds can see for themselves that God is fair and that we are worthy of heaven because Jesus has forgiven our sins and died in our place.

We've gone into a little background behind this loaded verse of Scripture. Go ahead and write your own paraphrase of it on your Scripture Sheet.

(Be prepared to review these points before the students paraphrase the verse on their Scripture Sheets. Encourage them to verbalize their questions and paraphrase them to you. It might be difficult, but it's part of the learning process.)

III. REVELATION 14:6, 7: FIRST ANGEL'S MESSAGE: THE GOSPEL TO EVERYONE; RESPECT GOD, GIVE HIM GLORY, AND WORSHIP HIM; THE JUDGMENT OF GOD HAS COME.

A significant portion of Scripture noted by Seventh-day Adventists is Revelation 14. This chapter contains three basic messages from three different angels. Let's look at the first message in Revelation 14:6, 7.

(Have one student read it, then open up discussion.)

(Note such phrases as "everlasting gospel" and "every nation, tribe, language and people" [NIV].

(What does "fear God" mean? How do we give God glory?)

(What does "the hour of his judgment has come" [NIV] mean?)

(What does it mean to worship the Creator?)

(Following the discussion, have students write their own paraphrase of the first angel's message on their Scripture Sheets. During this discussion, have someone unknown to the group barge in and interrupt the study by shouting, "Listen to what the three angels have to say!" Either focus on this interruption as an illustration of the "loud voice" element of the three angels' messages or act perplexed and then refer to this incident a little later.)

That's a very comprehensive message. It's for everyone and deals with the big realities of the entire universe. That's why the angels are described as shouting with a loud voice. It's like the interruption we experienced a few minutes ago. As Seventh-day Adventists we feel compelled to communicate this message boldly. If somebody wants to know what Christians are called to do, here it is in a nutshell. Are you willing to be part of getting out the word?

IV. REVELATION 14:8: SECOND ANGEL'S MESSAGE: GOD'S ENEMIES WILL LOSE.

The second angel's message is found in Revelation 14:8.

(Have one student read it, then open it up for discussion. Write paraphrases on the Scripture Sheet.)

Remember, we're reading a highly symbolic portion of the Bible. Babylon represents everything that goes against God. The root of Babylon can be found at the

Tower of Babel. It's the result of not trusting God and doing it yourself. Sometimes it shows itself in outright rebellion against God. The symbolic meaning of adultery is a failure to be faithful to God. When God's people follow other gods, it's referred to as spiritual adultery.

With this brief explanation, the message becomes clear: Those who are against God lose! Most people already know that. A few question it. Some think there's plenty of time before they need to make any decision or action about it. The question I have is Why be on the losing team? It's one thing to play hard in a simple game. It's another thing to know in advance who the winner and the loser will be in the ultimate showdown of all history. This is the biggest event in the universe, and you get to choose whether you will be on the winning team or the losing team! Is this a no-brainer or what?

In a sports championship some people will make predictions about who will win and who will lose. People even bet money on who they think will win. Let me share with you the predictions some made about a recent sports championship.

(Read the predictions made prior to a major sports event, such as the Super Bowl, the World Series, a championship boxing match, etc.)

Notice how certain these people sound, although everybody knows that anything might happen. There have been enough upsets to show us we can't predict with 100 percent certainty who will actually win.

But the second angel's message doesn't read like a bragging prediction or an analyst's guess. No, it's more like a statement based on fact. We read the reason for losing—leading people to leave God for other gods. The one who looked great—Babylon the Great—ends up being the loser in the bigger picture. For all the glamour and glitz associated with living apart from God, everyone can know it's the losing team. Which team are you on?

V. REVELATION 14:9: THIRD ANGEL'S MESSAGE: BAD NEWS FOR GOD'S ENEMIES; GOD'S PEOPLE WILL NEED PATIENCE.

We're ready for the message from the third angel in this trio. It's found in Revelation 14:9-12.

(Have one student read this, followed by discussion and paraphrases on Scripture Sheet 9.)

This message sounds rather ominous to me! For those who go against God, there will come a time when His patience and mercy give way to judgment and punishment.

We often hear about God's kindness and gentleness. Sometimes we're left with the impression that God would never punish anyone. But the enemies of God will discover that their fight has been against the God of the universe. The God who created them and died for them won't continue to allow Himself or His people to be taken advantage of because of His patience. Because God keeps providing opportunities for His enemies to choose His side, some think God's wrath will never be seen. But according to this third angel, that time will come.

God's people will need patience to hang on until that time. No doubt there will be times that it seems as if evil wins, as it mocks God's faithful followers. Loyalty gets tested when it appears that your side isn't making it. Are you committed to the point of hanging on when it doesn't look good and all you have are the promises that haven't yet been fulfilled? Can you believe messages from three angels during that time? Getting the message ahead of time certainly helps to anticipate those times of trouble. And this is part of the message too.

CONCLUSION:

This calls for serious commitment. Are you ready to be part of the team that gets out the messages from these three angels? It's a critical task against severe opposition and carries incredible consequences for everyone! Will you be part of the team that gets out the word—yes or no?

(Wait for students to respond. Help them identify where the battle is being fought in their sphere and how they can respond, including taking the offensive.)

Although we haven't yet seen God face-to-face, He has given us some rich symbols that tell us what He's like. The Old Testament sanctuary shows us some of the things Jesus does for us. In addition to dying for us, He forgives our sins, provides for our daily needs, gives us guidance, and intercedes for us. Our Judge is the one who died for us! What symbol from the sanctuary do you appreciate the most, and why?

(Allow students to respond.)

Let's close with a few moments of silent prayer for you to thank God for the reality of what the sanctuary represents; then I'll close with an audible prayer for our group as a whole.

(After a few moments of silence, offer a closing prayer.)

SCRIPTURE SHEET 9
The Sanctuary and the Three Angels' Messages

1. Hebrews 8:1, 2, 5:

What it means: _____

_____

2. Daniel 8:14:

What it means: _____

_____

3. Revelation 14:6, 7:

What it means: _____

_____

4. Revelation 14:8:

What it means: _____

_____

5. Revelation 14:9-12:

What it means: _____

_____

WORK SHEET 9
The Sanctuary and the Three Angels' Messages

1. What were the items in the desert sanctuary? (Basic drawing of the sanctuary, including the altars and pieces of furniture.)

2. **What do each of these items represent?**

   Altar of burnt offering _____

   Laver _____

   Table of shewbread _____

   Candlestick _____

   Altar of incense _____

   Ark of the covenant _____

   Courtyard _____

   First compartment _____

   Second compartment _____

FAMILY TALK BACK SHEET 9
The Sanctuary and the Three Angels' Messages

1. Since God can be with His people everywhere all the time, why did He want them to build a sanctuary?

2. If you were to boil down the messages and the symbols of the sanctuary to one sentence, what would you say?

3. The first angel of Revelation 14 has the everlasting gospel for all people. What would you say the *gospel* is? What part do you play in getting that message to all people? What part does your church play in this?

4. What do the following parts of the first angel's message (Revelation 14:6, 7) mean to you?
   > Fear God
   > Give glory to Him
   > The hour of His judgment has come
   > Worship the Creator

5. The second angel gives a message that God's enemies (Babylon) will lose. Where does it seem that God's enemies are winning right now?

6. God, especially in the New Testament, seems so forgiving, patient, and gentle. How does this relate to the description of what happens to His enemies in Revelation 14:9-11? Why do they get such serious punishment?

7. What does it mean to keep the commandments of God (Revelation 14:12)? What does it mean to have the faith of Jesus? Why does this require patient endurance?

Baptismal Bible Study Guide Outline 10

BAPTISMAL VOWS

Introduction: Baptism as a rite of passage; you're the one to be primarily responsible for your spiritual life now.

I. Baptismal vows (regular or simplified).
    A. Go over each baptismal vow.
    B. "I do" response for commitment/recommitment.

II. Question-and-answer time.
    A. Can be integrated throughout the study.
    B. Try to link responses to previous studies and additional Bible study.

III. Conclusion: Signing the baptismal vows.

Baptismal Bible Study Guide 10

BAPTISMAL VOWS

SCRIPTURE TEXTS:
There are no texts specifically for this study; however, be prepared to refer to previous studies or to respond to items not covered in these studies.

DECISION TIME:
Follow through on commitment for baptism by signing the baptismal vows.

MAKE IT CONCRETE (stage 3 appropriate):
Use simplified version of the baptismal vows for students to follow.

MATERIALS NEEDED:
One "study" set of baptismal vows for each student (a simplified version for better understanding).
One official set of baptismal vows for each student.
A pen for each student (for signing baptismal vows).

INTRODUCTION:
We've been through a number of Bible studies in preparation for your baptism. I realize that some of this was simply a review for you. You're fortunate to be part of a family that has brought you up to love God. Now you've come to the point of your life when you need to choose for yourself whether or not what others have chosen for you will continue to be your choice now. Your parents and others who have made these choices for you in the past will now function as your supporters.

You're not by yourself when it comes to your spiritual life, but you will now be the one primarily responsible for it. No matter how mature or spiritual you think you are, don't try to do this all by yourself. Being the one primarily responsible means you are the one who asks for help or support. It doesn't mean that you've got to live your Christian life alone. Part of being a member of the body of Christ is to rely on others, just as others will be relying on you.

Your baptism is a significant rite of passage toward adulthood. Some people think that once they are baptized, their spirituality is set for life. Nothing could be further from the truth. In fact, sometimes people find that things seem to get worse for them spiritually once they are baptized. In the great battle between Christ and Satan, your life will still be a battlefield after you publicly symbolize that you've given your life to Christ by being baptized. Being on Christ's side doesn't mean you're free of the devil; it means you now have the power of God to fight the devil. Welcome to combat! We will continue to need God, and we need each other, too.

What we're going to do in this session is to go through the baptismal vows. We'll take turns reading the baptismal vows as we go around the circle. Feel free to ask questions as we go along, and we'll also have an open question time at the end when you can ask any question about anything.

I'll give you the option of going through these vows either the way they appear on the official baptismal certificate or by using a simplified version that some pastors have developed.

(Have the students read through number 4 on the baptismal certificate and then number 4 on the simplified baptismal vows sheet. Once the students decide which set of vows to use, start with number 1 and go through each one, providing clarification where necessary and getting a nod and/or verbal agreement on each from the student. This is a great time for those who are already baptized to reaffirm their baptismal vows and for those not yet baptized to become familiar with the process.)

BAPTISMAL VOWS

(Updated at the 1995 General Conference session)

1. I believe there is one God: Father, Son, and Holy Spirit, a unity of three co-eternal Persons.
2. I accept the death of Jesus Christ on Calvary as the atoning sacrifice for my sins and believe that by God's grace through faith in His shed blood I am saved from sin and its penalty.
3. I accept Jesus Christ as my Lord and personal Saviour, believing that God, in Christ, has forgiven my sins and given me a new heart, and I renounce the sinful ways of the world.
4. I accept by faith the righteousness of Christ, my intercessor in the heavenly sanctuary, and accept His promise of transforming grace and power to live a loving, Christ-centered life in my home and before the world.
5. I believe that the Bible is God's inspired Word, the only rule of faith and practice for the Christian. I covenant to spend time regularly in prayer and Bible study.
6. I accept the Ten Commandments as a transcript of the character of God and a revelation of His will. It is my purpose by the power of the indwelling Christ to keep this law, including the fourth commandment, which requires the observance of the seventh day of the week as the Sabbath of the Lord and the memorial of Creation.
7. I look forward to the soon coming of Jesus and the blessed hope when "this mortal shall . . . put on immortality." As I prepare to meet the Lord, I will witness to His loving salvation by using my talents in personal soul-winning endeavor to help others to be ready for His glorious appearing.
8. I accept the biblical teaching of spiritual gifts and believe that the gift of prophecy is one of the identifying marks of the remnant church.
9. I believe in church organization. It is my purpose to support the church by my tithes and offerings and by my personal effort and influence.
10. I believe that my body is the temple of the Holy Spirit; and I will honor God by caring for it, avoiding the use of that which is harmful; abstaining from all unclean foods; from the use, manufacture, or sale of tobacco in any of its forms for human consumption; and from the misuse of or trafficking in narcotics or other drugs.
11. I know and understand the fundamental Bible principles as taught by the Seventh-day Adventist Church. I purpose, by the grace of God, to fulfill His will by ordering my life in harmony with these principles.
12. I accept the New Testament teaching of baptism by immersion and desire to be so baptized as a public expression of faith in Christ and His forgiveness of my sins.
13. I accept and believe that the Seventh-day Adventist Church is the remnant church of Bible prophecy and that people of every nation, race, and language are invited and accepted into its fellowship. I desire to be a member of this local congregation of the world church.

SIMPLIFIED BAPTISMAL VOWS

(Note: In leading young people through the baptismal vows, the author found that he had to paraphrase the statements so frequently that he prepared a simplified version of the vows. Over the years a number of other pastors have provided input regarding the wording and phrasing as a checkpoint to be true to the meaning of the original baptismal vows, while making them understandable to young people.)

1. I believe in God the Father; in His Son, Jesus Christ; and in the Holy Spirit.

2. I accept the death of Jesus to pay for my sins.

3. I accept the new heart Jesus gives me in place of my sinful heart.

4. I believe that Jesus is in heaven as my best friend and that He gives me the Holy Spirit so I can obey Him.

5. I believe God gave me the Bible as my most important guidebook.

6. By God living in me, I want to obey the Ten Commandments, which include the observance of the seventh day of the week as the Sabbath.

7. I want to help as many people as possible to be ready for the soon coming of Jesus.

8. I believe God gives special abilities to His people, and that the Spirit of Prophecy is given to His chosen people.

9. I want to help God's church with my influence, effort, and money.

10. I want to take good care of my body because the Holy Spirit lives there now.

11. With God's power, I want to obey the basic principles of the Seventh-day Adventist Church.

12. I want to be baptized to show people I am a Christian.

13. I want to be a member of the Seventh-day Adventist Church, and I believe this church has a special message to give the world.

CONCLUSION:

If you agree to take these vows, I invite you to sign your baptismal certificate. *(Close with a group prayer.)*

How to Make the Baptismal Service Positively Memorable!

When a person gets married, *whom* they marry is the *big* issue. *When* and *where* the marriage ceremony takes place are smaller issues, although they're still important.

Choosing to be baptized is like getting married to Jesus. The *big* issue is *why* one is choosing Jesus for oneself now. But there are still some choices about *when* and *where* that must be decided.

Most people are baptized in the baptistry at the church during the church service. This "prime time" gives more church members the opportunity to be a part of the baptism. While baptism is a testimony to others about one's commitment to Jesus, it also serves as an encouragement to others, including those who may not know the candidate very well.

Some people feel as though being baptized during the church service rushes this important ceremony. They want a separate service that makes the baptism the focal point. The person being baptized certainly should have major input in deciding *when* and *where* he or she will be baptized. Here are a few ideas to stimulate your thinking.

WHEN: **During the church service.**
WHERE: **At the church baptistry.**

1. The baptism may be included in a sermon about commitment to Christ, providing a tangible illustration of commitment and an application of how to respond.

2. The baptism may occur in place of the sermon, with follow-up testimonies about what other church members remember about their own baptisms.

3. The baptism may be the focal point of the first half of the church service, occurring in the middle of several songs of praise and commitment.

4. The baptism may occur during the first half of the church service, followed by a laying on of hands at the close of the church service and a prayer for the baptized person to receive the Holy Spirit.

5. The baptismal candidate is introduced to the church as one who has made the decision to be baptized. During the vote into membership, an invitation to stand can be extended to various interested groups, such as family members; followed by Sabbath school leaders and/or schoolteachers the candidate has had; then friends, fellow Sabbath school members, and classmates who are supportive of this decision; and finally, the entire church. In addition to the baptismal certificate, the pastor can present a memento (such as a rose) from the women's ministry group and a copy of *Steps to Christ* from the board of elders would be appropriate.

WHEN: A time other than the church service.
WHERE: At the church baptistry.

1. Friday night gathering, such as a vespers program.
2. Friday night following an agape feast. After the baptism observers may participate in a foot-washing service, then everyone can take part in a Communion service.
3. Following the church service and a potluck (or other meal), a separate program that focuses on the baptism could take place on a Sabbath afternoon at the church.
4. To coincide with a significant event that doesn't match the Sabbath calendar (birthday, conversion date, New Year's Eve, Christmas Eve, or when a significant relative, friend, or dearly loved pastor is in town). Although the Sabbath hours are an ideal time to conduct baptisms, they certainly do not have to be limited to Sabbath.
5. During Sabbath school, with the baptismal candidate's Sabbath school division focused on this event and what has led up to it. Other Sabbath school groups can finish their programs early to witness the baptism.

WHEN: At a time other than the church service.
WHERE: At a place other than the church baptistry.

1. Baptism in a lake. Water temperatures vary, as do lake bottoms. You may need to wear tennis shoes or thongs. A gentle slope into the water means the one being baptized will be a long way from shore, so a brief discourse from the shore is appropriate before heading into the water. The one being baptized should stand between the shore and the one who is doing the baptizing. The lake may have special significance prior to the baptism, and certainly will have additional importance following the occasion.
2. Baptism in a river. In addition to water temperatures and the river bottom, the flow of the current must also be considered. The head of the one being baptized should point upstream. Often a calm portion of a river can be located. Rivers can provide a lovely, scenic spot for a baptism. Even Jesus was baptized in a river.
3. Baptism in an ocean. This is usually much like baptism in a lake, depending on how active the surf is. Timing for immersion might be an issue. Saltwater also feels slightly different from freshwater.
4. Baptism in a swimming pool. A private pool can provide an intimate setting for a small baptism. Public pools can handle larger crowds and are sometimes used for mass baptisms.
5. Baptism in a portable baptistry. Some conferences have portable baptistries for use in conjunction with evangelistic series conducted where places to baptize are limited. The portable baptistry consists of a rigid frame with a waterproof lining to hold the water. Some type of stairway is needed for entering and exiting the baptistry.

A FEW THINGS PASTORS CAN DO:
1. "Practice" the baptism on dry land with the candidate. Although pastors may have conducted a number of baptisms, the baptismal candidate is new to this. There

are questions—how to hold one's hands, how not to get one's nose smashed, how long to be held under the water. What if my robe swooshes up and exposes my bathing suit? Do I bend at the waist, the knees, or arch my back? The water is easier than dry land, so practice a dry-land baptism before doing the real thing.

2. Have the candidate write a paragraph describing why he/she has chosen to be baptized at this time, and what this baptism means. This may be read by the candidate or the pastor in the baptistry.

3. Select a special text for each baptismal candidate and dedicate that passage to the candidate in the baptistry.

4. Have family and friends stand during the baptism in support of the person being baptized. Significant people, such as a youth intern or a schoolteacher, might also stand with the pastor in the baptistry.

5. Involve family and friends in supplementing the baptism by encouraging cards and gifts, a potluck, a special dinner, refreshments, or even sending invitations prior to the event. Note this as the new spiritual birthday for the baptismal candidate. This date can be celebrated in the future as the person matures in his/her Christian development.

Resources for Pastors

Handbook for Bible Study
A guide to understanding, teaching, and preaching the Word of God.
Includes reproducible exegesis work sheets for contextual, cultural,
structural, verbal, theological, and homiletical analysis. By Lee J.
Gugliotto. Hardcover, 432 pages. US$39.99, Cdn$57.99.

A Reason to Believe
The 27 fundamental beliefs have been condensed
to just 10 in this youth doctrinal/baptismal course:
divinity, rebellion, humanity, revelation, Jesus, response, love, joy, future, and purpose. Paper, 48
pages. Paper, US$4.99, Cdn$6.99.

How to Help Your Child Really Love Jesus
Hundreds of practical ideas from child development specialist Donna J.
Habenicht for helping children grow spiritually. Paper, 224 pages.
US$11.99, Cdn$17.49.

Guide's **Greatest Stories**
These gripping true stories of God's power represent
some of the best stories in the history of *Guide*. A
great resource for illustrations compiled by Randy
Fishell. Paper, 157 pages. US$8.99, Cdn$12.99.

Secrets From the Treasure Chest
Using God's Word, the writings of Ellen White, and personal experience, Charles Mills responds to tough questions kids ask about God,
homelife, school, relationships, and more. A devotional book for ages
9-12, it is also a valuable resource for issue-oriented talks. Quality
paperback, 381 pages. US$10.99, Cdn$15.99.

The Best of Creative Skits for Youth Groups
A valuable resource for youth workers who want lively feature presentations at
youth gatherings. Each easy-to-perform skit captures a vital aspect of the growing
Christian's life. By Randy Fishell and D. Gregory Dunn. Paper, 128 pages.
US$9.99, Cdn$14.49. Available spring 1997.

Available at all ABC Christian bookstores **(1-800-765-6955)** and other Christian bookstores. Prices
and availability subject to change. Add GST in Canada.

NOTES

NOTES

NOTES

NOTES

NOTES